ROUTLEDGE LIBRARY EDITIONS: SOVIET ECONOMICS

Volume 8

THE IMPACT OF SOVIET SHIPPING

THE IMPACT OF
SOVIET SHIPPING

SIMON BERGSTRAND
and
RIGAS DOGANIS

Routledge
Taylor & Francis Group

LONDON AND NEW YORK

First published in 1987 by Allen & Unwin (Publishers) Ltd

This edition first published in 2023
by Routledge
4 Park Square, Milton Park, Abingdon, Oxon OX14 4RN

and by Routledge
605 Third Avenue, New York, NY 10158

Routledge is an imprint of the Taylor & Francis Group, an informa business

© 1987 Rigas Doganis and Simon Bergstrand

British Library Cataloguing in Publication Data
A catalogue record for this book is available from the British Library

ISBN: 978-1-032-48466-2 (Set)
ISBN: 978-1-032-48659-8 (Volume 8) (hbk)
ISBN: 978-1-032-48663-5 (Volume 8) (pbk)
ISBN: 978-1-003-39014-5 (Volume 8) (ebk)

DOI: 10.4324/9781003390145

Publisher's Note
The publisher has gone to great lengths to ensure the quality of this reprint but points out that some imperfections in the original copies may be apparent.

Disclaimer
The publisher has made every effort to trace copyright holders and would welcome correspondence from those they have been unable to trace.

THE IMPACT OF SOVIET SHIPPING

SIMON BERGSTRAND & RIGAS DOGANIS

Transport Studies Group
The Polytechnic of Central London

London
ALLEN & UNWIN

Boston   Sydney   Wellington

**Allen & Unwin (Publishers) Ltd,
40 Museum Street, London WX1A 1LU, UK**

Allen & Unwin (Publishers) Ltd,
Park Lane, Hemel Hempstead, Herts HP2 4TE, UK

Allen & Unwin, Inc.,
8 Winchester Place, Winchester, Mass. 01890, USA

Allen & Unwin (Australia) Ltd,
8 Napier Street, North Sydney, NSW 2060, Australia

First published in 1987

British Library Cataloguing in Publication Data

Bergstrand, Simon
 The impact of Soviet shipping.
1. Merchant marine – Soviet Union
I. Title II. Doganis, Rigas
387.5'0947   HE847
ISBN 0–04–338143–X

Library of Congress Cataloging-in-Publication Data

Bergstrand, Simon, 1958-
 The impact of Soviet shipping.
Bibliography: p.
Includes index.
1. Merchant marine – Soviet Union.   2. Shipping – Soviet Union.
I. Doganis, Rigas, 1939-   II. Title.
HE847.B38   1987   387.5'0947   86–14146
ISBN 0–04–338143–X (alk. paper)

Set in 10 on 12 point Palatino by
Nene Phototypesetters Ltd, Northampton,
and printed in Great Britain by
Billing and Son Ltd, London and Worcester.

Contents

CONTENTS

ix

Preface

The Transport Studies Group of the Polytechnic of Central
London has long had an interest in the policy aspects of
international shipping. When in the late 1960s and 1970s flag
of convenience vessels were thought to pose a major threat to
western shipping interests, the Group investigated the phe-
nomenon of convenience registries and a number of reports
and papers were published. These showed that the impact of
convenience registries, later euphemistically renamed 'open
registries' was not always adverse and that the issues raised
were more complex than the press, shipowners or seamen's
unions sometimes suggested.

By the early 1980s the focus of controversy had switched to
the shipping activities of the communist countries of Eastern
Europe whose fleets appeared to be expanding. Since the
Soviet merchant marine operated the largest of these communist fleets it became the object of widespread criticism
from western shipowners and even governments. Such criticism was aimed mainly at the increasing size of the fleet, at the
extent and effect of Soviet competition in the maritime
markets and at the economic and commercial bases on which
the Soviet fleet operated. Yet little was known about the Soviet
merchant marine or the nature and extent of its activities.

In view of our long-standing interest in international
maritime policy issues we felt that this gap should be filled.
After some early research into Soviet shipping operations, the
Transport Studies Group was fortunate to receive a grant from
the Science and Engineering Research Council. This enabled
us to continue this research on a more full-time and systematic
basis. The present work also owes much to many people who
have helped either in tracking down data sources or by
discussing with us various aspects of Soviet shipping. They
are too numerous to mention by name. But we do owe a

special thanks to Dr Philip Hanson of the University of Birmingham who made valuable critical comments on some of our early work and to Ken Moore, lately of the General Council of British Shipping, who provided useful factual information and also pointed us towards other data sources. We would also like to thank the several Soviet shipping company officials and academics who gave up their time to discuss with us the workings of the Soviet shipping industry. Finally we are grateful to Maureen Cole for her patience in typing a difficult manuscript and complex tables with admirable accuracy.

Introduction

To the casual observer, Soviet merchant shipping represents a paradox. It is frequently portrayed as a major competitive threat to West European and North American shipowners. Yet at the same time other sectors of Soviet industry are derided for their inefficiency, poor management and technical backwardness. Is shipping unique among Soviet industries, able to take on the best the Western industrialized nations can offer and win, or is the threat more imaginary than real? This book sets out to resolve this paradox through a detailed analysis of the operations and impact of Soviet merchant shipping.

Criticism of Soviet shipping operations has come primarily from shipowners and relevant ministries in Western Europe and North America. In particular, Soviet shipping firms have been criticized for undercutting rates and oversupplying capacity in the liner trades, especially where they are cross-traders, and in the cruise markets. At the same time the Soviets have been repeatedly criticized, as in January 1986 by the French government, for ensuring that a disproportionately large share of their bilateral seaborne trade is carried on Soviet vessels. Western shipowners have gone beyond mere criticism of Soviet shipping practices. Many shipowners or shipowners' organizations, such as the General Council of British Shipping have attributed the decline of their own fleets partly to Soviet competition and have called for direct support from their own government or outright retaliation against the Soviets. The European Commission has taken up their case. In 1985 it established a group of five governments to monitor Soviet liner fleet operations and it is considering action to limit the operations of state-owned shipping companies.

One of the measures included in the Draft EEC Shipping

Policy formulated during 1985 and 1986 aimed to introduce a levy on freight rates charged by lines employing unfair pricing practices. The measure could be used against a line charging the lowest rates on a route if it enjoyed some form of uncommercial advantage such as state ownership and if there was evidence of damage or potential damage to EEC shipping lines.

The crux of the criticism made of Soviet shipping is that it does not operate on a strict commercial basis but that political, foreign exchange or strategic considerations outweigh commercial criteria in the decision-making process. The possibility that Soviet shipping costs might be lower in some real sense is ignored altogether. Because the commercial basis of Soviet shipping operations is poorly understood in the West a variety of reasons and arguments have been put forward by critics of Soviet shipping to explain why Soviet firms can so easily undercut established tariffs. These reasons, often interrelated, can be summarized as follows:

(1) The operating costs of Soviet vessels are lower because the basis of costing is different. Particular cost elements, such as depreciation, are excluded altogether or understated.

(2) The Soviet fleet is heavily subsidized by direct or indirect state funding.

(3) Soviet vessels do not have to meet normal commercial criteria. That is they do not have to cover their costs out of revenues.

(4) Earning foreign exchange through cross-trading is more important than covering the full costs of vessels engaged in such trades.

(5) At a political level it is sometimes argued that the trading activities of the Soviet merchant fleet are part of some grand political design to undermine Western shipping power.

There is also the additional question of the strategic value of the Soviet fleet. It is patently true that any state of some size, particularly a major power, would consider a merchant fleet to have considerable strategic and military potential. This was clearly illustrated during the recent Falklands War by the extensive use of merchant vessels by the British armed forces. It goes without saying that a large Soviet fleet is of strategic importance to the Soviet government. But do strategic factors outweigh all others when making decisions about the size or the commercial practices of the Soviet merchant fleet? This is an impossible question to answer with any certainty. It is likely that strategic considerations underlie the shipping policies of most large powers but do not determine the day to day operations of their merchant fleets. In the present analysis the issue of strategic considerations in shipping policy is left aside because such considerations are difficult to disentangle and because the Soviet Union is likely to be no different in this respect than any major maritime power. On the other hand, the Soviet system does allow for commercial and strategic considerations to be run together more easily than in the West. This is because with a centralized decision-making process the authorities can more readily take decisions on investments, provision of capacity, ship types and so on while allowing for non-commercial considerations of various kinds. The ability to do this is, after all, one of the claimed advantages of a planned economy.

The chapters which follow explore the nature of Soviet shipping activities and the degree to which they pose a real rather than an imaginary threat to the shipping interests of the traditional maritime states. This is done, first, through a detailed examination of the organization, characteristics and size of the Soviet fleet in relation to the Soviet Union's own requirements (Chapter 1–3), and then through a close analysis of Soviet activity in particular markets. The overall deployment of the Soviet fleet is analysed in Chapter 4, while Soviet participation in the liner trades is the focus of Chapter 5. Chapters 6 to 8 examine respectively the direct bilateral trades to and from the Soviet Union and Soviet activity in the bulk trades and in the cruise markets. Chapter 9 sets out to establish, as far as this was possible, the bases on which key commercial and operating decisions are made with Soviet shipping firms and the role played by non-commercial criteria mentioned above. The final chapter assesses the overall impact of Soviet shipping by pulling together the results of the analyses in the earlier chapters.

Data sources in English or Russian on Soviet shipping are limited, but the few sources available have been used where appropriate. Extensive original research has also been carried out using shipping and other data whose primary purpose may have been quite different. Most of this original research is contained in Chapters 4, 5 and 8. While there are a number of books dealing with the workings of the Soviet economy, little has been published about the basis of decision-making within Soviet shipping firms. The analysis of this aspect of Soviet shipping has been based partly on a series of discussions in London with Soviet shipping managers or visiting Russian academics and partly on the few publications available.

Despite any shortcomings in the data, the analysis which follows is the first exhaustive account of Soviet shipping which deals not only with the industry in terms of its size, vessel types and so on but also examines in detail the deployment and use made of those vessels in particular trades, the quality of service provided and the economic criteria used by Soviet shipping managers in taking key decisions.

CHAPTER ONE

The Organizational Framework of Soviet Merchant Shipping

1.1 The Basic Structure

The operations of individual Soviet shipping firms are constrained by the organizational framework of Soviet shipping. Its most characteristic feature is the attempt to maintain a high degree of centralized control. This is done through direct ownership of the fleet by the central government and through centralized planning. In practice, as will become evident later, the individual shipping manager can, within limits, exercise some degree of autonomy in decision-making.

There are four key elements in the organization of Soviet shipping. There is first of all the Ministry of Merchant Marine *(Ministerstvo Morskogo Flota)*, commonly known as Morflot, which effectively owns and ultimately controls the entire fleet. Under the ministry there are three regionally based holding corporations. These holding corporations each oversee a number of separate shipping companies based within their region. Finally there are a number of semi-autonomous corporations or agencies which are linked directly to the ministry (Figure 1.1).

1.2 The Ministry of Merchant Marine (Morflot)

Shipping firms in the Soviet Union were nationalized shortly

1

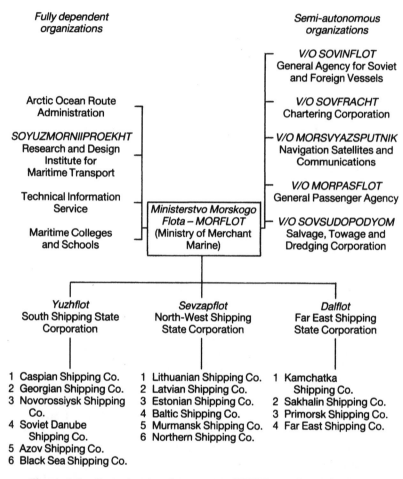

Figure 1.1 Organizational structure of USSR merchant shipping.

after the Revolution and subsequently were controlled by the People's Commissariat of Transport. In 1946 the ministry was formed to control all water transport including ports though some changes have since taken place. These include the removal of inland water transport to another ministry in 1954 (Boehme, 1983). The ministry is based in Moscow where it liaises with the relevant government departments such as foreign trade and shipbuilding. It is not entirely independent. Broad overall decisions on planning issues lie in the hands of

Gosplan, the state planning authority. Basic allocation of resources and general aims are therefore established at a level higher than the ministry itself.

The ministry produces general plans based on the resources made available to it through Gosplan and in accordance with its general aims. It also supervises and co-ordinates a range of activities related to shipping through its many departments. These issues are explained by the names of the departments of the ministry listed in Table 1.1 though there would appear to be some overlap between departments.

Table 1.1
Key Departments of Ministry of Merchant Marine

Foreign Relations Department
Protocol Department
Legal Department
Department for Shipbuilding Programme
Planning and Economics Department
Financial Department
Educational Institutions Department
Science and Technical Department
Department for Ships' Technical Supplies
Department of Food and Consumer Goods Supplies
Central Inspectorate of Safety of Navigation
Department for Shipping and Port Operations
Navigation and Maritime Communications Department
Department for Port Construction and Development
Engineering and Ship-repairing Department

1.3 The holding corporations

Direct Morflot control proved increasingly difficult during the rapid expansion of the Soviet fleet in the 1960s. In 1970 three regionally defined holding companies of 'state economic associations of maritime transport' were established with three key functions.

(1) To apply general plans to specific regional issues, and co-ordinating shipping in the area controlled.
(2) To improve the management system by taking it from central to region level.
(3) To handle new specialized transport requirements.

3

The firms are 'Sevzapflot' covering the north and west of the country, 'Yuzhflot' for the south and 'Dalflot', which has responsibility for the Far East. Each has its own budget and is responsible for a group of shipping companies. One of the corporation's main activities is to assess the requirements of each shipping company and then to attempt an optimum vessel allocation between them. Planning targets for each company come from the ministry but are handed down and supervised by the holding corporation. The latter would also co-ordinate the flow of information from shipping companies to the ministry for planning purposes.

To some extent the functional emphasis of each corporation is different. Dalflot has, as its prime task, serving the needs of the coastal areas of the Soviet Far East where the road and rail network is very thin compared with the rest of the country. Only 18 to 20 per cent of the corporation's activities are associated with foreign trade; a proportion much lower than Sevzapflot's. Yuzhflot specializes in tanker transport and as a result over half of total Soviet tonnage is under its control.

1.4 The shipping companies

There are sixteen shipping companies under the control of Morflot, each of which can be defined geographically or functionally. They vary greatly in size, the largest controlling twenty times the tonnage volume of the smallest (Table 1.2). Some sources refer to a seventeeth corporation called either the Central Asian Shipping Company or the Aral Sea Shipping Company. It is thought that this does exist to carry river/sea traffic in the Aral Sea area but because its trade is internal and does not involve a major sea, it is not under the control of Morflot.

Eleven are predominantly or entirely dry cargo operations while two, Novorossiysk and Primorsk, are tanker companies. Several have evolved from pre-revolutionary capitalist firms. Two examples are (a) the Caspian Shipping Co. which claims roots in the Kavkaz and Merkuriy Company established in 1858, and (b) the Danube Shipping Company which once bore the name Prince Yuriy Gagarin & Co. Some, such as the Baltic

Table 1.2

Trading Tonnage of the Soviet Shipping Companies, 1982

Shipping Company	Total			Tankers			Dry Cargo Ships		
	No.	Thou. GRT	Thou. DWT	No.	Thou. GRT	Thou. DWT	No.	Thou. GRT	Thou. DWT
YUZHFLOT									
1 Caspian	72	300	335	37	161	206	35	139	128
2 Georgian	49	531	807	37	312	461	12	219	346
3 Novorossiysk	126*	3,317	5,414	125*	3,298	5,382	1	19	32
4 Soviet Danube	62	237	269	1	—	—	62	237	269
5 Azov	130	599	783	1	2	2	129	597	782
6 Black Sea	245	2,638	3,702	3	125	139	242	2,513	3,563
SEVZAPFLOT									
7 Lithuanian	38	181	255	—	—	—	38	181	255
8 Latvian	107	945	1,287	58	740	1,067	49	205	220
9 Estonian	88	252	315	1	2	2	87	250	314
10 Baltic	171	1,217	1,636	—	—	—	171	1,217	1,636
11 Murmansk	61	478	681	—	—	—	61	478	681
12 Northern	147	573	806	3	5	5	144	568	801
DALFLOT									
13 Kamchatka	50	156	201	4	6	—	46	150	195
14 Sakhalin	78	318	406	—	—	—	78	318	406
15 Primorsk	54	352	499	54	352	499	—	—	—
16 Far-Eastern	226	1,405	1,825	—	—	—	226	1,405	1,825
Total	1,704*	13,499	19,221	323*	5,003	7,769	1,381	8,496	11,453

* The figure includes 10 combination carriers totalling 625,143 grt or 1,085,952 dwt owned by the Novorossiysk Shipping Company. Figures may not total due to rounding.

Source: Soviet Shipping (Supplement to *Morskoi Flot*), vol. 3, no. 3 (1983).

Shipping Company, were formed soon after the Revolution and others after the Great Patriotic War (for example, the Latvian company in 1945).

The most recent companies were formed from subsidiaries of larger firms. For example the Far East Shipping Company set up a tanker subsidiary at Nakhodka in 1969. Three years later this became the independent Primorsk Shipping Company. Similarly the Novorossiysk Shipping Company was the tanker department of the large Black Sea company until 1967.

The Novorossiysk company is the largest in tonnage terms with around 5 million dwt of tankers and ore/bulk/oil carriers (OBOs). Much of its activity concerns the provision of Soviet industry with oil, including fuel supplies for fishing fleets. It is also largely responsible for carrying Soviet seaborne oil exports. Shipments of oil products to Cuba, India, Vietnam and North Europe are also important. The company operates to a small extent on the open market and vessels are to be found on ore trades from South America and Canada to Japan, the Mediterranean and the northern continent. Such trips can provide useful back cargoes for an outward voyage of oil to Cuba. Tankers have also been chartered by major oil companies such as Shell and Agip.

The other tanker company, Primorsk, is only a tenth of the size of the Novorossiysk and is mainly engaged in internal trade. Coastal trade accounts for 80 per cent of tonnage carried and much of the remainder comprises oil and oil products shipped to Japan and South-East Asia, especially Vietnam (Soviet Shipping, 1984). The firm has built up a good reputation for cross-trading products such as animal fat and vegetable oil around the Pacific and now wins annual contracts for such business. The president of the company has claimed that Soviet participation in the trade has recently been damaged by Japanese involvement in US anti-Soviet strategy.

Each regional holding corporation controls one very large dry cargo shipping company. These are the Baltic, Black Sea and Far East Shipping Companies known respectively as BSC, Blasco and Fesco. Each has well over one million tonnes gross of shipping and all of the largest liner vessels are divided among them. The controversial cross-trading lines discussed

6

in later chapters, such as Balt Orient and Besta, are part of these companies.

One of the more specialized firms is the Northern Shipping Company which is primarily engaged in exporting timber. Its 152 vessels are nearly all ice-classed and carry unitized planks and pulp from Northern Russia. Exports are primarily to Western Europe, plus North Africa and Cuba. On the return trip to the North vessels carry supplies to the communities along the coasts of the White, Barents and Kara Seas along with heavy construction equipment. Vessels are chartered out on the open market in late winter when some of these areas are unnavigable because of ice and exports are reduced.

Another firm in a similar situation is the Sakhalin Shipping Company. The substantial share of its business is domestic cargo to the Eastern Arctic, Chukotka, Magadan District, the Kuriles and Sakhalin. Its major export cargoes are timber, pulp, paper and woodchip, with much going to Japanese timber importers. Return cargoes include Japanese steel, consumer goods, chemicals and motor vehicles. The company also operates a train ferry service with eight vessels. There is a total of eighty trading ships in the fleet.

The Murmansk Shipping Company also serves local primary industry. It originally exported timber and fish from the White Sea and has more recently added apatite, iron ore and other metals to its cargoes. Like the other northern firms it faces problems of ice, shallow water and a swampy shoreline. As a result the vessels used by these firms tend to be small and with ice-classification. Icebreakers, river/sea general cargo ships and Arctic multi-purpose vessels are to be found in their fleets. Although they export raw materials from the home base they have little involvement in cross-trading. The Murmansk company, for example, only operates the small Arctic Line from Germany to Canada.

Each Soviet shipping company is to some extent self-supporting in having its own balance sheet and independent budget. It extends this self-support through involvement in peripheral activities including port operations and ship repair. Each Soviet shipping company is responsible for most of the ports in its area so, for example, the Baltic Shipping Company (BSC) operates Leningrad, Kaliningrad and others.

BSC also runs ship repair yards including four floating docks (Seatrade, 1976). Dredging and salvage firms are generally subsidiaries of the shipping companies.

There is extensive co-operation between the companies within each holding corporation with regards to ports and ship repair. For example, the various Yuzhflot companies have 24 repair yards between them and through preplanned schedules they can not only maintain each others' vessels but also take on some foreign flag work.

1.5   Semi-autonomous agencies/organizations

1.5.1   *Sovinflot and overseas agencies*

Sovinflot, the general shipping agency of the Soviet Union, was established as late as the 1960s. Its dual role is to act as a general agent for foreign ships calling at Soviet ports and to link the varies agencies in non-Soviet ports which provide services to Morflot vessels. Its responsibilities include arranging stevedoring, provision of tugs and other port services as well as bunkering contracts. Bunkers are sold to foreign vessels in Soviet ports. Abroad Sovinflot contracts with oil majors such as Shell, BP, Mobil and Exxon to supply Soviet vessels.

The various foreign shipping agents used by Soviet lines often have some Soviet equity participation or, as in Britain, they may be wholly Soviet owned. The Anglo-Soviet Shipping Company handles the general agency and commercial aspects and Sovinflot has the majority shareholding. Morline, a subsidiary of the above was established in London in 1976 and handles the liner side of the business.

Similarly in the United States, Morflot American Shipping Inc. (Moram) acts as a general agent and is wholly owned by Sovinflot. More commonly joint equity exists, in some cases because this is required by law in the country concerned. In Japan for example the United Orient Shipping Agency has its shareholding split as follows:

8

	Shareholder	%
Soviet	Sovfracht	25
	Soviet Far East Shipping Co.	25
Japanese	Yamashita-Shinnihon	40
	Azuna Shipping Co.	10

It is thought that Morflot would have preferred sole own-ership (Boehme, 1983).

Equity participation by Soviet shipping companies in shipping agencies is common. In Benelux the Transworld Marine Agency, a large organization with 11 branches includ-ing 2 in Germany, was established in 1970 to handle Soviet business. Its equity participation includes 3 Soviet shipping companies (Table 1.3).

Joint participation is also found in the agencies throughout the continent as well as in Australia, Canada and Japan. Around twenty examples have been identified with Soviet participation ranging from 35 to 95 per cent of equity.

Table 1.3
Equity Participation in Transworld Marine Agency (Belgium)

	Shareholder	% share
Soviet	Sovfracht ⎱ Sovinflot ⎰	33
	Baltic Shipping Co. Murmansk Shipping Co. Latvian Shipping Co.	42
Belgian	Vloeberghs Steinman Co.	20
	Mr Pierre Stoop	5

1.5.2 Sovfracht

The Soviet Union has various shipping requirements which cannot be fulfilled by its merchant fleet. There are also periods when certain Soviet tonnage is surplus to requirements. Sovfracht is effectively a chartering monopoly which operates to meet these eventualities.

Before it was established in 1929 various buying and selling agencies and departments had arranged their own transport. It was hoped that centralization would mean that better terms could be achieved. Sovfracht was originally part of the Ministry of Foreign Trade *(Ministerstvo Vneshnaii Torgovli)* but it was later transferred to the merchant marine ministry.

As the Soviet Union's only broker it covers all chartering in and out through six departments: Baltic, South, Atlantic, Far East (which includes Indian and Pacific Oceans), timber and tanker. There is also a variety of service departments such as planning, agency, and accounts. Its Moscow operation is supplemented by Sovfracht (London) Ltd. which works on the Baltic Exchange. This is the main subsidiary although there are others, some wholly owned (such as Sovfracht USA Inc.), some with foreign participation (as in Paris) and others operating as joint ventures, for example, the Genoa office.

Some aspects of the activities of Sovfracht in the dry cargo and tanker markets are examined in Chapter 8.

1.5.3 Other organizations

Among other Soviet organizations linked to shipping are Sojuzvneshtrans and Morpasflot. The former handles transit cargo passing throughout the USSR as well as internal transport of imports and exports. Morpasflot is the general passenger agency. Although passenger ships generally belong to the various shipping companies, agency duties are handled separately. In some cases, such as in the UK, separate tour operators have been established. CTC, a subsidiary of the Anglo-Soviet Shipping Company, runs cruises on Soviet ships but they are effectively supervised by Morpasflot (see Chapter 8).

Finally, not all Soviet merchant shipping is under the control of Morflot. A separate Ministry of the Fishing Fleet manages the massive Soviet fleet of fishing vessels and fish factories and some small ships such as tenders belong to other ministries. Of the 23.8 million gross tonnes on the Soviet register, around 7 million is associated with the fishing industry and one million is managed by neither Morflot nor the Fishing Ministry (Morskoi Flot, 1985).

CHAPTER TWO

Demand for Soviet Shipping

2.1 Soviet international trade

It is generally accepted that the primary function of the Soviet merchant marine is to meet the foreign trade requirements of the country. The Ministry of Foreign Trade has a number of corporations or agencies which buy and sell abroad and almost all foreign trade is controlled by them. The minor exceptions mainly concern barter deals involving frontier areas, for example, Leningrad–Finland (Nove, 1980). In a centrally planned economy it is essential that foreign trade is controlled and that the internal economy is isolated from external influences. Attitudes and policies towards international trade have changed throughout Soviet history. As a result, corresponding trade levels and shipping requirements have altered accordingly. Stalinist policies tended towards self-sufficiency but postwar trends emphasized trade with the rest of the Eastern Bloc, particularly as a result of the formation of the Council for Mutual Economic Assistance (CMEA or Comecon) in 1949. Initially this created a requirement for short-sea shipping to supplement land links but with the accession of Cuba (in 1972) and more recently of Vietnam there has been some requirement for deep-sea intra-CMEA trade. Thus, until relatively recently the pattern of Soviet trade has not been one which demanded a substantial deep-sea fleet. This has implications for the current shipping requirements of Soviet trade in terms of tonnage, type of vessel and overall fleet size.

In signing the UNCTAD Code of Conduct for Liner Conferences the Soviet Union accepted cargo sharing. It would therefore be expected to limit its merchant fleet of general cargo and container ships to one which would be capable of carrying 40 to 50 per cent of the Soviet Union's international liner cargo trade plus whatever was required for domestic trade. Likewise, its commitment to bilateral shipping agreements and qualified support for bulk cargo sharing would be expected to result in plans to provide Soviet tonnage for up to 50 per cent of international requirements in the bulk sectors plus the tonnage needed for domestic traffic.

By examining the pattern and volume of Soviet international trade by sea and comparing it with the Soviet merchant fleet available for such trades it is theoretically possible to determine in which sectors, if any, the Soviet Union is an over-provider of tonnage. If surplus Soviet tonnage can be found in particular sectors then one would expect that competition with Western and other shipping countries to be most likely in those sectors.

But there are problems in attempting to determine shipping requirements through examining trade figures. These centre around the form of the statistics, though there is the added problem of seasonality which might mean more vessel tonnage being required than would be apparent from annual statistics. In the analysis which follows, three sources of trade statistics have been used:

(1) the annual volumes produced by the Soviet Ministry of Foreign Trade – *Vneshnyaya Torgovlya SSSR;*
(2) United Nations Coastal Area Statistics from the *Monthly Bulletin of Statistics;*
(3) national statistics of some countries with which the Soviet Union trades.

The Soviet annual volume of trade statistics is produced promptly, five or six months after the period it covers. Imports and exports are broken down by detailed categories using a Soviet commodity coding system and useful summaries are given. Unfortunately, figures are given in roubles plus, for some commodities, a measure of quantity or volume. The problem is that in the Soviet Union domestic prices do not reflect either scarcity or abundance and cannot be used as meaningful indicators of value. In official statistics, foreign trade or 'valuta' roubles are used and these have nothing to do with internal rouble prices. As Nove (1980) explains, 'transactions with Western and most developing countries are undertaken in Western currencies, which are then converted into roubles at the official rate ... Trade within Comecon is conducted at prices based loosely on world prices of the recent past, ostensibly cleansed of speculative fluctuations ... prices for the same items can vary quite widely'. Thus trade levels measured in roubles may not adequately represent the true value, in terms of world prices, or the volume of the trade involved. They can only be regarded as rough indicators of the relative importance of trade between those countries exporting to and importing from the Soviet Union.

For some commodities (less than half of the entries in *Vneshnyaya Torgovlya SSSR za 1984g*) quantities or volumes are also given. Unfortunately no country has a full set of such figures and, because of inconsistency in the units of measurement, they are of little use anyway. Some commodities are measured in tonnes, others in metres, square metres, cubic metres, and so on. In a few cases, such as furs, the figures are for the number of items.

It is not just Soviet national trade statistics which are difficult to use. Data from Soviet trading partners are also in many cases inadequate as far as making deductions about shipping needs is concerned. It should be added that other countries are often much slower than the Soviet Union at generating such data. This means that there are no satisfactory data on tonnage movements from Soviet ports to other countries. One useful source, however, provides data on a trading area basis throughout the world. The United Nation's *Monthly Bulletin of Statistics* for September 1984 included a 65 page list of cargo movements (in tonnes) by sea analysed by commodity classes and coastal areas.

Rather than identifying countries the data are presented for geographical groups such as North America East Coast or the Caribbean. Soviet trade appears in three groups:

13

(a) Centrally Planned Europe – Baltic Sea (comprising East Germany, Poland and Soviet Baltic ports);
(b) Centrally Planned Europe – Black Sea (comprising Bulgaria, Romania and Soviet Black Sea ports);
(c) Centrally Planned Asia (comprising Vietnam, China, Democratic People's Republic of Korea and Soviet Pacific ports).

Soviet trade must dominate within the first two of these groups and form a significant part of the third. The importance of China as a contributor to the latter grouping should be noted.

What comes out most clearly from UN cargo movement figures for 1981 (Tables 2.1 and 2.2) is the dominance of relatively short trade links, especially for exports, in the trade patterns of the centrally-planned economies. A substantial proportion of *exports* (Table 2.1) from the coastal areas under consideration is taken up with cargo flows from the Baltic and Black Seas to European or Mediterranean destinations. In fact 86 per cent is destined for ports in North Europe or the Mediterranean; or for ports elsewhere in the Baltic and Black Seas. In the Far East, 81 per cent of exports from Centrally Planned Asia go to the Far East or South-East Asian coastal areas or go elsewhere in the Centrally Planned Asia Group. Japan is the major destination.

By comparison to these shorter trade links deep-sea export trade flows from the centrally planned economies are relatively small. The only major long-distance flow was that to the Caribbean which totalled over six million tonnes. This was dominated by USSR to Cuba trade, much of it originating from the Black Sea ports. The latter area also exported three and a half million tonnes to South and South-East Asia, much of it to Vietnam. There were also some smaller export flows to North and South America. But overall, the United Nations figures suggest that the export trades of the centrally planned economies do not require a large deep-sea fleet.

The situation with *imports* is rather different. Although there are flows over short distances, particularly from North Europe and within the Black Sea, there are also massive imports from North and South America and Oceania. About

14

Table 2.1
Destination of Exports by Sea from Centrally Planned Economies
1981 (000s tonnes)

Coastal area of destination	Exports from centrally planned economies of:		
	Baltic Sea	Black Sea	Asia
North America	530	1,680	1,842
Central America and Caribbean	1,189	5,006	33
South America	1,715	173	1,680
North Europe	44,156	3,767	2,155
Centrally Planned Europe	7,263	22,302	122
Mediterranean	2,673	38,790	778
East and West Africa	114	102	89
Red Sea/Persian Gulf	251	3,820	538
South and South-East Asia	465	3,516	4,553
Centrally Planned Asia	186	0	396
Far East	183	191	26,426
Oceania	11	91	197
WORLD Total	58,971	79,438	38,809

Note: Trade for which destination is unknown is included in totals.
Source: UN (1984).

43 per cent of the imports of the Baltic centrally planned economies come from the Americas, North, Central and South. For the Black Sea centrally planned economies the figure is 39 per cent; for those in Asia 46 per cent come from the Americas. Another 16 per cent of the imports of the Asian group come from Oceania, mainly Australia. These large volumes include grain imports from Argentina, Australia, Canada and the United States.

In order to appreciate the implications of this trade analysis it is necessary to look more closely at three of the larger deep-sea trade routes, one involving imports to the Soviet Union and the other two relating to both import and export trades. On the Soviet import side, the trade from North America, both east and west coast, is analysed in Table 2.3. Both Canada and the United States are among the largest trading partners of the centrally planned economies especially with the Soviet Union. It is clear from the analysis that much

Table 2.2
Origin of Imports by Sea to Centrally Planned Economies 1981
(000s tonnes)

Coastal area of origin	Imports to centrally planned economies of:		
	Baltic Sea	Black Sea	Asia
North America	8,834	14,555	18,293
Central America and Caribbean	3,884	687	754
South America	14,521	13,073	617
North Europe	18,543	4,152	2,845
Centrally Planned Europe	7,915	21,652	186
Mediterranean	5,862	10,864	962
East and West Africa	2,745	714	36
Red Sea/Persian Gulf	731	1,665	275
South and South-East Asia	619	4,498	3,900
Centrally Planned Asia	119	3	396
Far East	56	856	7,736
Oceania	54	438	7,023
WORLD Total	63,883	73,157	43,025

Note: Trade for which origin is unknown is included in totals.
Source: UN (1984).

Table 2.3
North American Exports to Centrally Planned Economies, 1981
(000s tonnes)

To centrally planned economies of:	From North America:				Cereals as % of total
	East Coast		West Coast		
	Total	Cereals	Total	Cereals	
Baltic Sea	8,091	7,039	743	659	87
Black Sea	14,032	10,880	523	474	78
Far East	10,385	8,200	7,908	5,486	75

Source: UN (1984).

of this trade is in cereals. It would, therefore, require medium-sized bulk carriers to carry it.

As previously pointed out, one of the largest long-distance trade flows from the centrally planned economies is that to the Caribbean. There is also substantial return tonnage. Most of

Table 2.4
Trade between the Caribbean and Centrally Planned Economies,
1981 (000s tonnes)

| Commodity | To Caribbean from: | | From Caribbean to: | | |
	Baltic Sea	Black Sea	Baltic Sea	Black Sea	Far East
Total	1,151	5,001	3,845	683	708
of which:					
Sugars	0	0	3,655	647	708
Crude petroleum	0	5,000	0	0	0
General cargo	943	1	11	36	0

Source: UN (1984).

the cargo on the routes is from the Soviet Union and 80 per cent of it is in the form of crude oil from the Black Sea ports to Cuba, thus indicating the need for a tanker service. Much of the rest of the flow is in the form of general cargo (Table 2.4). In the opposite direction 96 per cent of the flow is sugar, requiring smaller, specialist bulk carriers.

Another major deep-sea trade is with South Asia (Pakistan, India, Sri Lanka, Bangladesh, Burma and the islands of the Indian Ocean). The largest item here in volume terms is metalliferous ores from South Asia, accounting for 57 per cent of the Baltic trade and 94 per cent of that to the Black Sea. This again is a trade requiring bulk shipping facilities (Table 2.5).

Table 2.5
Trade between South Asia and Centrally Planned Economies,
1981 (000s tonnes)

| Commodity | To South Asia from: | | | From South Asia to: | | |
	Baltic Sea	Black Sea	Far East	Baltic Sea	Black Sea	Far East
Total	221	3,178	706	527	4,297	263
of which:						
Metal ores	0	0	0	300	4,045	0
Crude petroleum	0	2,610	0	0	0	0

Source: UN (1984).

2.2 Shipping needs of international trade

The above analysis suggests that the required fleet composition for these centrally planned economies dominated by the Soviet Union, if they wished to be self-sufficient in shipping, would include a large fleet of smaller general cargo vessels to serve short-sea links to the major trading partners. There would also be a large number of medium-sized bulk carriers to import grain, ore and other major bulks. Tankers for oil exports would also be required. Combined carriers such as OBOs would be an alternative.

This impression is to some extent confirmed by an analysis of major trading partners in value terms. As Table 2.6 shows, three-quarters of Soviet trade is with Europe. That is with the EEC, EFTA, other Western Europe countries, plus Centrally Planned Europe which together total 73 per cent of total trade. By contrast, Europe accounts for a little over half of UK trade. If other short-sea links, specifically North Africa, Near East and

Table 2.6
Soviet Foreign Trade by Trading Bloc, 1984 (million US$ FOB)

Bloc	Imports	Exports	Total trade	% of Total
Developed market economies				
EEC	10,295	18,837	29,132	17
EFTA	5,050	5,576	10,626	6
Other Europe	3,795	4,190	7,985	5
Other developed	8,412	1,472	9,884	6
Developing economies				
Africa	2,405	1,763	4,168	2
America	6,248	5,023	11,271	7
Middle East	1,943	1,430	3,373	2
Asia	2,842	3,024	5,866	3
Centrally planned economies				
Asia	1,877	3,491	5,368	3
Europe	37,615	39,913	77,528	45
Total	80,624	91,649	172,273	(96)

Note: Values of trade for which country of origin or destination could not be attributed are included in the totals.
Source: UN (1985).

Table 2.7
Major Soviet Trading Partners Excluding Eastern Europe,
1984 (million roubles)

Country	Soviet exports	Soviet imports	Total
West Germany	4,224	3,277	7,501
Cuba	3,752	3,464	7,216
Yugoslavia	3,062	2,755	5,817
Finland	2,421	2,307	4,728
Italy	3,156	1,325	4,481
France	2,447	1,773	4,224
USA	306	2,829	3,135
Japan	840	2,054	2,894
India	1,537	1,272	2,809
UK	1,393	819	2,212
Total top ten trading partners	23,138	21,875	45,017
Total Soviet trade	74,384	65,327	139,711
Top ten as % total trade	31	33	32

Source: *Vneshnyaya Torgovlya SSSR za 1984g.*

Far East, are added, the predominant need for vessels suited to this type of trade is clear. Overland links are obviously important for trade with Eastern Europe but they also apply to some of the other top trading partners. As Table 2.7 shows, West Germany, Yugoslavia and Finland take first, second and third places among the non-CMEA countries and each has major road and rail links with the Soviet Union.

The Soviet Union has few large trading partners at any great distance from the country. Its top ten trading partners account for a third of its international trade (45 out of 140 billion roubles in 1984). Of these ten only Cuba, USA and India require deep-sea shipping services to maintain the link.

A breakdown of Soviet foreign trade by mode of transport for two recent years shows that only half goes by sea. Nearly a quarter uses rail transport; a similar quantity travels by pipeline and river. Road and air traffic is insignificant in tonnage terms (Figure 2.1). A gradual increase in the importance of seaborne international trade can be identified. In 1980 only 47.6 per cent went by sea but by 1983 this had risen to 51.6 per cent. This can be attributed to the trend away from intra-CMEA trade.

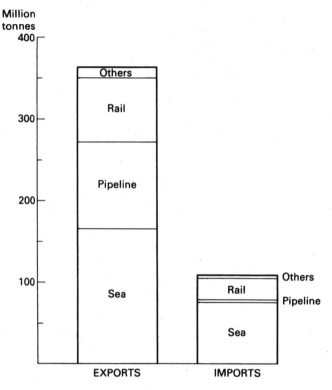

Figure 2.1 Soviet trade by mode of transport, 1984.
Note: 'Others' category comprises river, road and air transport.
Source: Vneshnyaya Torgovlya SSSR za 1984 g.

2.3 Soviet internal trade

The transport sector of the Soviet Union has been influenced
by several basic government policies. Imperial Russia had
developed as a major trading nation particularly of primary
produce to Europe, and the early railway network reflects this.
During the post-revolutionary decade there was relatively
little trade except imports of machinery and corresponding
exports of raw materials with which to pay for them. There
then followed a long period characterized by the basic
objective of the first Five Year Plan, published in 1929; the
creation of a self-sufficient and economically independent

industrial base. This aim can be traced back to Lenin's writings in 1918 (Lenin, 1950).

This policy has a number of transport implications among which was the fairly low priority given to shipping because of the aim of self-sufficiency. Before the Revolution, much Russian trade was carried in foreign ships. Despite the low priority of shipping the communist regime at least enabled the Soviet Union to carry a larger share of its limited international trade in its own vessels. But the inward emphasis appears to have predominated as great stress was placed on domestic coastal and intercoastal traffic (Hunter, 1968). This policy survived throughout the Stalinist period and a marked growth in external trade did not occur until after 1954. Even now foreign trade is a relatively small contributor to national income.

Another basic policy which has influenced Soviet transport concerns industrial location. Again, going back to the 1920s, there were two clear aims: to locate industry more evenly; and to move industry closer to sources of fuel and raw materials (Hunter, 1968). To some extent these are contradictory and the latter aim has had more success. This has had implications for coastal shipping. In a general sense coastal shipping is characterized by the movement of low value, high volume raw materials and fuels. If these are refined or semi-finished at source, the demand for coasters is reduced. For the Soviet Union, however, the sheer size of the country, the distribution of resources and the nature of the inland transport system has led to the need for a substantial coastal fleet.

Over a third of cargo tonnage carried by Soviet vessels is coastal and the level has varied little over the last few years (Table 2.8). This is an important figure to bear in mind when assessing the size of the Soviet flag fleet and its potential impact.

In recent plans a major thrust of maritime development has been the development of cargo and support vessels for Siberian and Arctic exploration. Vast areas lack road and rail communications yet contain abundant natural resources; Siberia is thought to contain 85 per cent of Soviet fuel reserves and it is probable that additional substantial reserves also exist in the Arctic. There are many examples of industry

21

Table 2.8
Coastal Tonnage on Soviet Vessels

Year	Coastal traffic (million tonnes)	Coastal as a % of total traffic on Soviet vessels
1977	78.8	35.8
1978	82.6	36.0
1979	78.6	34.7
1980	77.7	34.0
1981	80.2	35.9
1982	79.9	35.6
1983	82.0	34.4
1984	82.4	35.0

Source: *Morskoi Flot*, various years.

exploiting these resources being located in Siberia, creating a demand for construction materials and equipment, plant and machinery, components and supplies in the area. Demand for shipping services has also developed through the need to support a rapidly growing population in these areas. In cases where economic development has not been at the raw material source, shipping services are required to export, for example, oil, nickel, copper and timber. One of the causes of the rapidly growing demand for vessels in Siberia and the Arctic is the extension of the navigation season brought about by technical advances.

It is only relatively recently that the Deputy Minister of Merchant Marine considered all year round navigation in many parts of the north viable. The navigational improvements planned in 1980 showed an 'extra profit' to local industry of 72 million roubles, while additional costs to the merchant marine including the work of all the icebreakers was 23 million roubles (Lloyd's List, 11 March 1982).

In summary, until the mid-1950s the Soviet Union did not require a large merchant fleet for its international trade. Since then international trade has grown rapidly but remains peculiarly localized, largely because of intra-CMEA trade but also because of the ability of Finland, West Germany and Japan to supply much of the bought-in technology of the Soviet Union. For its coastal and intercoastal trades the country required a substantial volume of tonnage during its isolationist period. More recently, Arctic and Siberian exploitation has stimulated demand for specialized tonnage to serve dispersed industries and populations in areas lacking any other transport facility.

In determining the vessel types apparently in demand to meet Soviet trade requirements, attention must be paid to bulk exports and imports. Oil, oil products and gas account for half of Soviet exports. Despite the importance of pipelines there is clearly a need for a tanker and gas carrier fleet. Imports of grain and sugar create a demand for a substantial number of medium and handy-sized bulk carriers. Trade in machinery and equipment is, at least on the import side, largely with neighbouring or European states. It could be assumed, therefore, that a general cargo and containership fleet would be dominated by smaller, short-sea vessels.

CHAPTER THREE

Supply of Soviet Shipping

3.1 The growth of the Soviet fleet

Soviet national and international trade creates a demand for transport links the nature of which would be expected to be a function of the form of trade in terms of commodity types and volumes, distance, required speeds and whether or not a land link can be maintained. A centrally planned economy such as that of the Soviet Union should be capable of closely matching transport and trade. As trade is centrally planned and controlled, transport systems can be designed to meet its requirements. A graph of the value of Soviet external trade since the Second World War exhibits three stages. Until 1960 a period of substantial growth existed; this slowed down during the 1960s but accelerated rapidly in the 1970s (Figure 3.1).

Contemporaneously, there were three phases of merchant fleet development. During the 1950s the worldwide growth of merchant shipping was rapid but the Soviet fleet exhibited little more than a 50 per cent increase in tonnage from two to three million tonnes gross. Consequently its position in the league of major merchant fleets fell from eighth to thirteenth (Table 3.1). The second phase was characterized by very rapid growth. In the late 1950s the fleet stood at about three million tonnes. In the ten years from 1960 to 1970 Soviet tonnage grew almost fivefold reaching close to 15 million grt by 1970. This rapid growth pushed the Soviet fleet up to sixth in the world. Relatively rapid growth continued till the mid-1970s. The third stage of Soviet fleet development from the mid-1970s

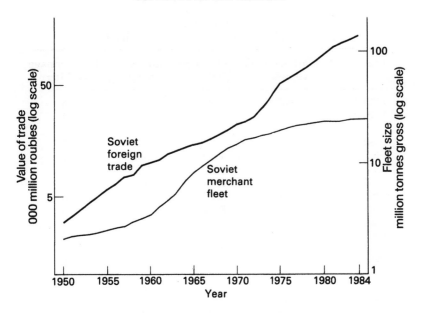

Figure 3.1 Growth of total Soviet trade and of the Soviet fleet
1950–1984 (logarithmic scale).

Sources: Vneshnyaya Torgovlya SSSR za 1984 g; Lloyd's Register of Shipping,
Statistical Tables.

onwards is characterized by a dramatic drop in growth rates.
This is especially so in the five year period after 1980. Between
1980 and 1985 Soviet tonnage grew by only 5.5 per cent. The
Soviet fleet is now fifth largest in the world after Liberia,
Japan, Panama and Greece. If open registry tonnage was allocated to countries of beneficial ownership, using UNCTAD
figures, the Soviet fleet would probably be ranked seventh.
The larger fleets would be Greece, USA, Japan, UK, Norway
and Hong Kong.

In retrospect, Soviet shipping policy since 1975 appears
more sensible than that of many Western shipowners. While
many of the latter continued to order substantial newbuilding
despite the worsening crisis and the increasing numbers of
vessels laid up, the Soviet policy has been one of ordering new
vessels either to replace vessels being scrapped or to meet
specialist needs. As a result the Soviet tonnage has increased
only very slowly in recent years and the Soviet share of world

25

Table 3.1
Growth and Ranking of the Soviet Merchant Fleet

Year	Number of vessels	Gross tonnage (000s)	Annual % change	World tonnage ranking
1950	967	2,125		8
1955	1,158	2,506		11
1960	1,138	3,429		13
1961	1,212	4,066	18.6	11
1962	1,313	4,684	15.2	11
1963	1,432	5,434	16.0	8
1964	1.674	6,958	28.0	6
1965	1,845	8,238	18.4	6
1966	2,024	9,492	15.2	6
1967	2,238	10,617	11.9	6
1968	4,206	12,062	13.6	6
1969	5,622	13,705	13.6	6
1970	5,924	14,832	8.2	6
1971	6,575	16,194	9.2	6
1972	6,851	16,734	3.3	5
1973	7,123	17,395	4.0	6
1974	7,342	18,176	4.5	6
1975	7,652	19,236	5.8	6
1976	7,945	20,668	7.4	6
1977	8,167	21,438	3.7	6
1978	7,991	22,262	3.8	6
1979	8,120	22,900	2.9	5
1980	8,279	23,444	2.4	6
1981	7,867	23,493	0.2	6
1982	7,713	23,789	1.3	5
1983	7,753	24,549	3.2	5
1984	7,095	24,492	−0.2	5
1985	7,154	24,745	0.1	5

Source: Lloyd's Register of Shipping, *Statistical Tables.*

tonnage has declined since 1970 (Figure 3.2). Such a policy is consistent with having a highly centralized and planned economy. The primary aim of the Ministry of Merchant Marine is to match the supply of shipping to the demand particularly in respect to the Soviet Union's own internal and bilateral trade needs. Speculative building of vessels for the relatively uncertain and unstable cross-trades would be inconsistent with the basic philosophy of a centralized

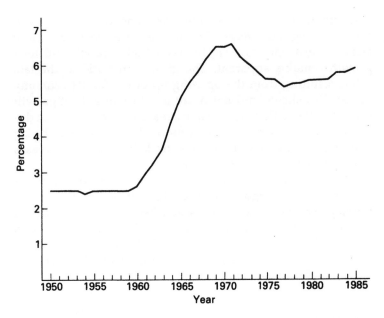

Figure 3.2 Soviet tonnage share of the world merchant fleet.
Source: Lloyd's Register of Shipping, *Statistical Tables.*

economy. Moreover, the Soviet view appears to have been that at a time of substantial overtonnaging it was not even necessary to have a merchant fleet that would cover 100 per cent of their own needs since there was so much surplus tonnage which could be chartered in cheaply. This was certainly the view expressed by the president of Sovfracht, the Soviet chartering agency (Maslov, 1984). The evidence seems to support this for the Soviets have, over many years, chartered in large numbers of vessels to carry their grain imports rather than build their own ships (Chapter 7 below).

The phases of Soviet trade and fleet growth do not match very closely. The rapid growth in trade found in the 1950s and 1970s was met not with a corresponding fleet growth but with very slow development. Comparatively sluggish trade growth in the 1960s was met with rapid fleet expansion (Figure 3.1). A partial explanation is that the figures used are of trade value. Comparable figures of trade volumes have proved difficult to obtain but the patchy data of trade volumes suggest that there was substantial growth in the 1960s and that this slowed down during later years. This matches the fleet data more closely. Nevertheless a lag between trade growth and fleet growth remains apparent. The growth in trade in the late 1950s resulting from the opening up of the Soviet economy under Khrushchev did not result in substantial fleet growth until the 1960s. This is more like a feature of the capitalist dry cargo market than one of state central planning in that the lag is typical of those found between trade booms and increases in shipping tonnage in the West.

Of course sea transport is not the sole means for exporting and importing cargo. Less than half of Soviet exports in tonnage terms now go by sea largely because of the growth of oil and gas pipeline traffic (Figure 2.1). The share of shipping in Soviet freight transport has in fact declined over the last few years in terms of tonne–kilometres from over 13 per cent in 1975 to under 12 per cent in 1983.

3.2 Pattern of growth

The development of the fleet over a period is determined by the inherited fleet size to which is added newbuildings and second-hand purchases; and from which is subtracted vessels sold, condemned, broken up or lost through casualty. After the Second World War the Soviet fleet was a hotchpotch of prewar vessels, Lease–Lend acquisitions and vessels taken in reparation. The rapid growth of the 1960s resulted from deliveries of simple and small vessels built to standard designs and delivered in larger numbers, substantially from shipyards in Eastern Europe. By the early 1980s supplies of newbuildings had become more varied, though CMEA countries still dominated. As the later 1984 order-book showed, 210 of the 257 vessels on order were to be built in centrally planned countries. A further 39 were Finnish buildings, leaving just eight vessels from other countries. But by 1986 the Soviet orderbook had diminished. There were only 153 vessels on the list of which 89 were being built in Comecon countries, 28 in Finland, 14 in Yugoslavia and the remainder elsewhere in Europe (Table 3.2). The simpler vessels are usually built in

Table 3.2
Soviet Ships on Order by Country of Building as at October 1984
and April 1986

Country			Vessels on order	
			1984	1986
CMEA	Bulgaria		18	3
	Czechoslovakia		29	1
	East Germany		36	8
	Poland		31	48
	Romania		34	6
	USSR		39	23
		sub-total	187	89
Others	Denmark		3	1
	Finland		39	28
	Portugal		3	5
	Singapore		2	0
	Yugoslavia		23	14
	Greece		0	4
	Malta		0	8
	Spain		0	4
		sub-total	70	64
		Total	257	153

Source: Fairplay, *World Ships on Order*, October 1984 and May 1986.

Soviet shipyards while those demanding intermediate technology and expertise are ordered from Poland. Specialist vessels including icebreakers and other Arctic vessels are more likely to be built in Finland, often as part of larger trade agreements. Interestingly the Soviet Union unlike other major shipping nations has rarely ordered new vessels from Far East shipyards in Japan or Korea but has consistently favoured European yards.

No clear pattern of vessel orders has emerged. As Table 3.3 shows, there are periods with no new orders and other periods of large-scale contracting. In the second quarter of 1983, for example, 45 vessels totalling nearly half a million deadweight tonnes were ordered. In the fourth quarter of the same year there were no new contracts. The order-books continue to be dominated by conventional general cargo vessels. A phase of container ship orders in 1981 and 1982 was

29

Table 3.3
New Soviet Vessel Orders by Year

Year	Dry cargo No.	thou. dwt	Dry Bulk/OBO No.	thou. dwt	Ro-Ro/ferries No.	thou. dwt	Container No.	thou. dwt	Tankers No.	thou. dwt	Total No.	thou. dwt
1978	12	113	3	143	—	—	5	31	4	229	24	516
1979	14	95	1	38	1	5	—	—	9	108 (5)	25	246 (5)
1980	18	236	1	20	2	36	—	—	15	255	36	547
1981	23	113	5	93	1	20	10	141	—	—	39	367
1982	38	186	3	200	19	78 (9)	7	112	3	21	70	597 (9)
1983	31	363	3	59	9	19 (5)	4	37	15	105	62	583 (5)
1984	18	115	—	—	—	—	3	73 (1)	6	399	27	587 (1)
1985	12	71	—	—	6	70	4	40 (3)	17	270	39	451 (3)

Notes: (1) For 1978 to 1981 the years are from November to October. In 1982 Fairplay rationalized their listings so that full calendar years now appear.
(2) These tables exclude passenger and miscellaneous vessels.
(3) Figures in parentheses are numbers of vessels of unknown deadweight.
Source: Fairplay, World Ships on Order, quarterly listing by Fairplay Publications.

followed by a trend towards roll-on roll-off ships in late 1982 and 1983. There are notably very few dry bulk carriers on order.

The size of the Soviet fleet is determined not only by newbuildings and purchases but also by the level of losses through casualty and vessels scrapped or broken up. In this respect it is worth noting that the Soviet fleet has an excellent safety record with one of the lowest rates of loss in the world. The annual loss rates have varied between zero and 0.1 per cent of the fleet over the twelve years to 1984. This compares with a world total loss rate of 0.27 per cent to 0.54 per cent (Lloyd's, *Casualty Returns*). No more than three vessels have been lost through casualty in each of the last twelve years and the worst figure was for 1984 when three ships aggregating 43 thousand tonnes were totally lost. These levels assume that all total losses are reported through Lloyd's Register of Shipping. Casualties occurring in and around Soviet ports may not appear.

The rate of fleet reduction through scrapping is substantially higher than the loss rate. The 1981–5 Five Year Plan stressed that merchant fleet development would be characterized by improving the quality and efficiency of the vessels rather than by rapid expansion. Replacement of obsolete tonnage was to be a priority. In fact scrapping levels are still low compared with traditional maritime states and the world as a whole. Until 1979 very few vessels were scrapped but during the period 1979–84, 0.33 to 1.0 per cent of the fleet was broken up annually. Although this is high by Soviet standards (Figure 3.3), it should be noted that worldwide, 1.4 to 4.0 per cent of all merchant shipping was scrapped annually during the same period. This programme has involved relatively few trading vessels. Of 234 vessels identified as having been broken up in 1982 and 1983 only 68 were trading vessels (some of these were in fact broken up earlier than 1982 but not reported until then). The majority were trawlers, whalers, fish carriers and factories. It should be added, however, that in terms of vessel numbers the split between trading and non-trading vessels scrapped is proportionate to the share of such vessels in the fleet as a whole. There is a risk that scrapping data from Lloyd's Register may also be incomplete. Evidence of scrap-

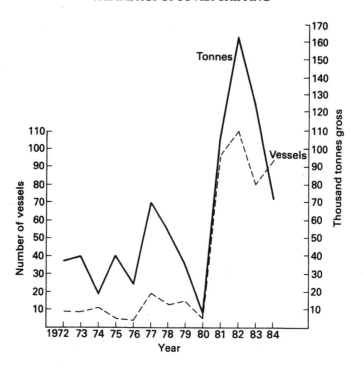

Figure 3.3   Soviet vessels broken up, 1972–84.

pings being recorded well after the event is to be found in some of the quarterly issues of Lloyd's *Casualty Returns,* so more vessels may have been scrapped but not yet reported. It is also possible that some Soviet vessels which were scrapped have not appeared in the Lloyd's data at all. There must be a number of extremely old vessels in the fleet if this is not the case.

Early in 1986 Morflot sold around thirty vessels for scrap in one of the largest deals of its kind ever seen. In a complicated transaction the ships were sold to a Cayman Islands company and placed under the British flag for their final voyage to Chinese breakers yards for a price of US $100 to US $118 per light displacement tonne. Twenty of the vessels were steam tankers built in the 1960s and around 50,000 tonnes deadweight each. The ten remaining vessels were general cargo ships of around 16,000 tonnes each.

Table 3.4
Soviet Ships on Order as at April 1986

Vessel type	Number on order	Aggregate dwt (where available)	Average dwt
Dry cargo	36	332,245	9,229
Container	10	140,873	17,609
Bulk carrier	2	134,640	67,320
Tankers	28	434,650	15,523
Passenger/ferries	15		
Supply ships	29		
Survey/research	13		
Dredgers	4		
Icebreakers	8		
Others/unknown	8		
Total	153		

Source: Fairplay, *World Ships on Order*, May 1986.

As mentioned above, the stated aim of Soviet fleet development in the 1980s has been to improve the quality and efficiency of the fleet by replacement of obsolete tonnage. Much of what has been scrapped from the trading fleet has been in the form of general cargo, ore carrying and tanker tonnage. In other words, vessels able to take on a variety of roles possibly in competition with other flags. What has replaced it has, to a large extent, been more specialized. The evidence suggests that a large number of Soviet vessels ordered in recent years have been specialist types (Table 3.4). These have included rail ferries for the Caspian Sea, accommodation barges for Siberia, LPGs specializing in ammonia transport and refrigerated ships designed to import bananas from Cuba. Recent deliveries have included many vessels for use in the Arctic such as ice-strengthened tankers and tugs, and nuclear icebreakers. River/sea vessels, often for use in Siberia, have included shallow draft icebreakers and tug/barge systems, ice-strengthened river/sea general cargo ships and suction dredgers. The Soviet research ship fleet, the largest in the world, has also been augmented by more hydrographic vessels and multi-purpose ships capable of oceanographic, seismic, navigational and meteorological research.

Many recent Soviet deliveries and new orders are for non-trading vessels. But even the trading vessels are, in some cases, highly specialized. A class of nine vessels being built by Wartsila of Finland is typical. These are 20,000 dwt Arctic multi-purpose vessels which can be used for transporting general cargo, rolling cargo, containers, grain, coal or ore. They work independently in very low temperatures and are therefore equipped with winches, hatches and hydraulics of special construction. The vessel can discharge cargo directly on to ice with transfer to the shore via a 38 tonne capacity hovercraft (Lloyd's List, July 1983). Such vessels, although they could be classed as a general cargo type, are clearly highly specialized. It is unlikely that they would ever be employed as competitors to or members of an international freight conference, as to do so would be to underutilize their capabilities considerably. It should be noted that such vessels would be listed as general cargo ships in Fairplay data (Table 3.4) despite their specialist nature. Clearly much of what has been ordered and built in recent years has been constructed for a specific route or purpose, often related to Soviet internal requirements. General purpose vessels, as opposed to multi-purpose ones, have been replaced by ships built for certain specific tasks. It could be argued that potential for competition with Western firms has been reduced as a result.

In contrast, some newbuildings are more obvious potential competitors because of their high productivity compared with what they replace. At the outset of containerization fully cellular vessels were claimed to be five times as productive as general cargo vessels of the same size. Today they would be considered at least three times as productive. By replacing a certain tonnage volume with new ships of the same tonnage the effective capacity of the fleet may be greatly increased. The Soviet fleet has no very large container ships but does include substantial numbers of efficient smaller cellular vessels such as the Khudozhnik class and many roll-on roll-off vessels. Over fifty container and Ro-Ro vessels were ordered between 1981 and 1983 (Table 3.3).

Overall, the growth of the Soviet merchant fleet appears broadly in line with the growth of Soviet external trade. If anything fleet growth is slipping back as pipelines carry large volumes of liquefied exports. As there is now more trade beyond CMEA countries a larger increase in shipping tonnage may have been expected since road or rail transport is not a feasible alternative to the more distant destinations. At the same time, increased vessel productivity could mean that the same volume of tonnage would, over a period, carry a greater volume of freight.

3.3 The nature of the Soviet fleet

The result of Soviet policy on vessel acquisition and disposition is a fleet with an unusual profile in terms of age, vessel type and vessel size. This is apparent when comparisons with the total world fleet and with the UK are made. The average vessel size for the Soviet fleet, at 3,500 gross tonnes, is much smaller than the world total at 5,400 tonnes (Table 3.5). This is despite the fact that Soviet non-trading and miscellaneous trading vessels are larger than the world average. Soviet oil tankers are, on average, less than half the size of those elsewhere. Ore and bulk carriers are well below the world average size. General cargo and container vessels are also much smaller than similar types worldwide.

Table 3.5
Average Vessel Size in Soviet, UK and World Merchant Fleets, 1985

Vessel type	Average size (000 gross tonnes)		
	USSR	UK	World
Oil tankers	10.8	22.9	21.9
Ore and bulk carriers	15.2	31.1	22.0
General cargo	4.6	2.6	3.6
Container ships	12.5	28.7	18.2
Other trading vessels	22.3	17.6	14.7
Total trading vessels	6.9	12.8	10.6
Non-trading vessels	1.8	1.2	0.8
Total fleet	3.5	6.0	5.4

Notes: (1) 'Other trading vessels' includes chemical tankers, gas carriers, bulk/oil carriers, passenger/cargo ships and vehicle carriers.
(2) 'Non-trading vessels' includes fish factories, fishing vessels, ferries, supply ships, tugs, dredgers, icebreakers, etc.
Source: Lloyd's Register of Shipping, *Statistical Tables* (1985).

Table 3.6
Composition of the Soviet, UK and World Fleets, 1985

Vessel type	% of fleet tonnage		
	USSR	UK	World
Oil tankers	19	40	32
Ore and bulk carriers	9	15	26
General cargo	31	9	18
Container ships	2	11	4
Other trading vessels	4	13	11
Total trading vessels	65	88	91
Fish factories and fishing vessels	27	1	3
Other non-trading vessels	8	11	6
Total non-trading vessels	35	12	9
Total fleet	100	100	100

Source: Lloyd's Register of Shipping, *Statistical Tables* (1985).

A partial explanation for its small average vessel size is that the Soviet fleet contains high proportions of vessel types which are, by their nature, small (Table 3.6). The Soviet fleet has a larger share of non-trading vessels than any other in the world. As much as 35 per cent of total tonnage falls into this category compared with 9 per cent worldwide, around 6 per cent for the fleet of the EEC countries and 2 to 3 per cent for the

Table 3.7
Vessel Types in the Soviet, UK and World Trading Fleets, 1985

Vessel type	% of trading fleet tonnage		
	USSR	UK	World
Oil tankers	29	45	35
Other tankers	0	3	2
Liquefied gas carriers	1	6	3
Bulk/oil carriers	4	7	6
Ore and bulk carriers	14	17	29
General cargo and passenger/cargo	48	10	19
Container and lighter vessels	4	12	5
Vehicle carriers	0	0	1
	100	100	100

Source: Lloyd's Register of Shipping, *Statistical Tables* (1985).

major flags of convenience. The main cause of this anomaly is that the Soviet Union has a huge fishing fleet. Over a quarter of its total tonnage is accounted for by fish factories, carriers, canneries and fishing vessels. Surprisingly 80 per cent of the world fleet of 872 fish factory ships flies the Soviet flag as does 38 per cent of all fishing tonnage. As well as these the non-trading category includes icebreakers, of which the Soviet Union controls over half, and ferries. Only Japan has a larger ferry fleet; even the substantial UK fleet is now smaller than the Soviet one.

If one excludes fishing and other non-trading vessels this profile of small ships is accentuated by the disproportionately large number of conventional general cargo vessels. These account for half of the trading fleet whereas worldwide less than a fifth of the trading fleet is composed of general cargo vessels (Table 3.7). In the case of the British fleet, general cargo vessels represent only one tenth of the total tonnage.

The Soviet fleet is conspicuously low on other types of tonnage as a result. Only 14 per cent of Soviet trading tonnage forms dry bulkers compared with the world figure of 29 per cent. Container vessels take up 4 per cent of the fleet compared with 12 per cent in the UK, 25 per cent in West Germany and 17 per cent in the United States. The Soviet fleet also has comparatively few gas carriers, products tankers and bulk/oil tankers.

While many American and Far Eastern shipowners have ordered specialized tonnage with container capacity of 3,000

Table 3.8
Age Profiles ot Total Soviet, UK and World Fleets, 1985

Age group (years)	% of gross tonnage		
	USSR	UK	World
0–4	15	14	19
5–9	20	27	26
10–15	19	40	31
15–19	23	12	14
20 and over	23	7	10
	100	100	100

Source: Lloyd's Register of Shipping, Statistical Tables (1985).

to 4,000 TEU or even more as a way of reducing the unit costs of transportation, an analysis of Soviet container vessels shows that they are relatively small by current standards. This is so even for Soviet newbuildings. The maximum capacity of Soviet cellular container ships has been kept below 1,000 TEUs and that of Ro-Ro ships at around 1,400 TEUs (Tables 4.4 – 4.6 in Chapter 4). Soviet ship managers feel that vessels of this size better match the requirements of the Soviet Union's external trade and in the cross-trades it is easier to fit such vessels into the gaps left by the large capacity vessels operated by Western companies. Thus the concentration on smaller-size vessels is deliberate Soviet policy rather than a failure to grasp the economic advantages of larger vessels (Maslov, 1984).

The Soviet fleet has also an unusual age profile (Table 3.8). As explained earlier in this chapter rapid fleet growth occurred in the 1960s. The vessels launched during this period are now 15 to 25 years old and therefore beyond what in the West would be their normal book life. In effect 46 per cent of the Soviet fleet is over 15 years old compared with 19 per cent of the UK fleet and 24 per cent of the world fleet. Within the Soviet fleet there is some variation. Its tankers are particularly old, over half being over 15 years, though recent scrapping will have altered the balance somewhat. By comparison its dry bulk fleet is young with 88 per cent being under 15 years (Table 3.9).

Compared with other major fleets the Soviet fleet is much

Table 3.9
Age Profiles of Soviet Oil Tanker and Dry Bulk Carrier Fleets, 1985

| Age group (years) | Oil tankers | | Bulk carriers | |
	Thou. grt	%	Thou. grt	%
0–4	599	13	605	20
5–9	1,221	27	1,261	42
10–14	407	9	766	26
15–19	955	21	261	9
20 and over	1,409	30	81	3
Total	4,591	100	2,974	100

Source: Lloyd's Register of Shipping, Statistical Tables (1985).

older and composed of smaller vessels. A very high proportion of the trading fleet, about half, is made up of relatively small general cargo vessels. The fleet as a whole appears deficient in the more modern types of vessels such as liquified gas carriers, OBOs and container ships and although some newbuildings on order are aimed at filling this gap, the overall composition of the Soviet fleet is unlikely to change appreciably in the next few years. In particular the new tonnage on order (Table 3.4) appears insufficient to allow for the scrapping of a sufficiently high number of very old vessels. The Soviet fleet will continue to be relatively old and from this point of view not very competitive.

3.4 Cargo trends

During the early 1980s the Soviet fleet carried between 220 and 230 million tonnes of cargo annually. The level appears to have peaked in 1983 at 238 million tonnes. Most of this is foreign trade where the share carried by the Soviet fleet has been increasing. By 1983 the Soviet lines were carrying about 60 per cent of the Soviet Union's seaborne foreign trade which totalled 229.5 million tonnes. The remaining 40 per cent or 92.5 million tonnes was carried by foreign vessels. Additionally 82 million tonnes of coastal traffic and 19.1 million tonnes of cross-trade cargoes were carried on Soviet vessels (*Soviet Shipping*). This suggests that only about 8 per cent of the tonnage carried by Soviet vessels was in the cross-trades. In terms of revenue, however, the contribution of cross-trading is likely to be much higher both because distances are greater and in many cases freight rates may be relatively higher. A Soviet source has suggested that between 20 per cent and 25 per cent of Morflot's earnings are from cross-trading.

The trend in Soviet cross-trading appears to be downward. In 1979 38 million tonnes was carried by Soviet vessels on cross-trades. This appears to have been the peak year. Since then cross-trade tonnage was halved in just four years to around 19 million tonnes. This figure is not large compared with other traditional maritime states but unusually the

Soviet Union combines an element of cross-trading with the carriage of well over half of its own foreign trade. While, as noted above, Soviet vessels carried in 1983 around 60 per cent of their country's seaborne trade, the British fleet carried only 25 per cent of the UK's seaborne trade.

CHAPTER FOUR

Soviet Fleet Movements and the Extent of Cross-Trading

4.1 Establishing the extent of cross-trading

Western criticism of Soviet shipping has centred to a large extent on the cross-trading activities of Soviet dry cargo vessels and liners. It is therefore important to establish to what extent the Soviet fleet is actually involved in cross-trading rather than in bilateral trade and the nature of such cross-trading. To do this one needs to monitor the movement and deployment of those Soviet vessels most likely to be involved. It is not necessary to monitor all Soviet flag vessels for though there are 7,154 ships in the Soviet fleet only 2,351 are trading vessels. Of these 435 are tankers of one form or another. The activities of the old and small tanker fleet are of little concern to Western shipping interests and are discussed briefly elsewhere (Chapter 7). What remains is a fleet of 1,916 actively trading dry cargo vessels. It is here that there is greatest potential for competition with the West.

However, more ships can be eliminated from the analysis. In particular, small dry cargo vessels can be excluded because in the Soviet Union these are likely to be restricted to coastal and river transport. Although short-sea activity, particularly to North Europe, may be a possibility they will not be deployed on longer routes. It is not possible to draw the line at any particular size of the vessel to distinguish between coastal shipping and international trade. For the present analysis only vessels over 3,000 gross tonnes have been monitored. One reason for this was to keep the number of vessels down to a manageable figure. What remains can be described as the fleet of Soviet trading vessels over 3,000 gross tonnes excluding tankers and passenger vessels. The data on 1,400 pages of print-out covered the movements of 1,297 such vessels during 1983.

Two analyses were carried out. First, the port to port movement of all these vessels was monitored for a year and the nature of each vessel's activity determined; then, the majority of the better and more modern liner tonnage was subjected to a detailed examination of movements. The aim of the analysis was to determine the nature of the trading pattern of each of the major Soviet vessels in the fleet. A key fact to establish was the number of vessels involved solely in Soviet direct trade with other countries compared with those that were cross-trading. It was apparent, however, that few vessels had a clear cut pattern of activity for the whole year.

4.2 Data problems

To obtain basic data on individual vessels, their ports of call and their sailing patterns during 1983 use was made of Lloyd's Shipping Information Services. But the incomplete nature of the data provided some problems. Some vessels thought to exist did not appear in the Lloyd's data. There are a number of possible explanations for this. Some could have been laid up for the whole year although Soviet sources deny that any of the fleet is in this condition. Alternatively, some may have been scrapped but not yet reported as such. Certainly Lloyd's *Casualty Returns* can be very slow in identifying scrapped ships, particularly of the Soviet flag, though this is not likely to account for many examples. A more probable reason is that vessels not appearing simply had not been recorded because they had been restricted to ports without Lloyd's agents. Only the main Soviet ports such as Leningrad and Kaliningrad in the Baltic or Vostochny and Nakhodka in the Far East appear in the data. Arguably this explains most omissions from the

Lloyd's data but since such vessels are essentially engaged in Soviet coastal trade this is not serious.

The data was also incomplete in that many vessels 'disappeared' for long periods. Some did not record a movement until well into the year. Some had no recorded movement for several months. These gaps normally occurred after arrival at or departure from a larger Soviet port. Refitting, maintenance and repairs will explain some gaps. In the West a maintenance period of around a fortnight would not be uncommon for a liner though most of these gaps in the schedule are for longer periods. Again there is the possibility of lay-ups. Alternatively vessels may have been waiting to load particular consignments. Perhaps the most likely explanation of gaps in the schedule is that the vessel has spent periods sailing between Soviet ports for which no reports have been provided via Lloyd's agents. Coastal and internal trade amounts to about 80 million tonnes annually, a third of all cargo shipped, so the capacity required to move it is considerable. Soviet sources claim one third of Soviet liner tonnage is employed in internal trading (Maslov, 1984). It is reasonable to expect that some vessels are involved in unrecorded coastal trade for part of the year while many vessels sail exclusively on internal services.

Another problem was identifying the reason for a call at a particular port. For example, a vessel sailing from one foreign port to the Soviet Union making a call of short duration at another port may be putting in for bunkers or other supplies or may be loading or unloading cargo. There were certain cases where the call was fairly obviously for bunkers. A common one was at the Canaries on the return from Latin America to the Soviet Union. Another was at Ceuta at the entrance to the Mediterranean. Some vessels on set routes made freak diversions for no apparent reason. For example, a vessel on the North Europe–Australasia trade suddenly diverted to Manila in the Philippines for one short call before sailing back to Australia and continuing with its normal itinerary. Establishing the nature of a call in some Soviet ports also caused problems. If a vessel was, at one end of a route, serving a range of North European ports plus a Soviet one was the Soviet call for crew changes, supplies or bunkers, or was it to load cargo? It has been assumed in most cases that a ship would not sail the length of the Baltic just to bunker or change crew so short calls have been assumed to be to load cargo. But where a longer call of several days duration is made it could still be either a maintenance call or a cargo oriented call.

In numerous cases a ship was recorded as sailing from a particular port then as returning to it without having called at another port en route. Where the sailing is from and back to a major Soviet port it was assumed to be going to a smaller Soviet port and the call went unrecorded. However, in some cases a vessel would leave a Black Sea port, sail out of the Black Sea, then sail back in leaving little time for a call elsewhere and with none being recorded. Given this sort of difficulty it was necessary to define carefully what sort of movement pattern fitted into each category. The following rules were followed.

A vessel engaged in *Soviet direct bilateral trade* would exhibit a movements record including a large number of calls at Soviet ports interspersed with calls at one or more ports in a non-Soviet range. (A port range is a set of all the ports between the two points along a coastline.) Generally non-Soviet calls would account for no more than two-thirds of the total. A vessel calling at foreign ports in different ranges between Soviet calls would not be counted as engaging in direct trade.

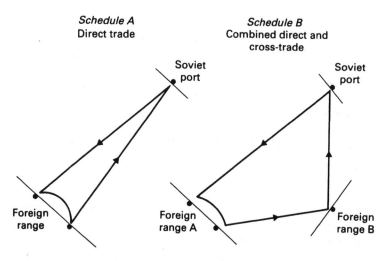

Figure 4.1 Direct and combined trading patterns.

It would instead be considered to be combining direct Soviet trade with cross-trade cargoes carried between the ranges (Figure 4.1). The only exception to this rule would be occasional bunker calls.

A vessel was assumed to be *cross-trading* if it sailed from one non-Soviet range to another without calling at a Soviet port. The only exception was an occasional brief Soviet call on an otherwise regular non-Soviet itinerary. Major Soviet cross-trading liner services such as Balt Orient are known to visit Soviet ports infrequently and are not thought to carry cargo originating in or destined for the Soviet Union.

A large proportion of the fleet did not fit in to either of these categories. A vessel calling regularly at a Soviet port and others nearby before sailing to a destination would appear to be *combining cross-traded cargo with direct trade*. A common example was Leningrad–Hamburg–Bremen–non-European port range–Bremen–Hamburg–Leningrad. In this case Soviet exports could possibly have been discharged in North Europe but it seemed more likely that the vessel would be loading for the non-European range. So a combined cross-trade/direct trade category was required. Vessels falling into it may in fact have been predominantly involved in *either* cross-trading *or* direct trade.

Gaps in the schedule posed a further problem. If for a particular vessel no movement was recorded for substantial periods which together totalled six months or more of the year, it was considered that there was *insufficient data* to decide on the nature of that vessel's trade. In fact it is likely that this indicated that the vessel had spent a substantial period engaged in Soviet internal trade.

4.3 Pattern of Soviet trading

The results of the analysis of vessel deployment show that about half of the main Soviet vessels were engaged solely in direct trade between the Soviet Union and other countries (Table 4.1). Hardly any vessels were engaged solely in cross-trading though a quarter of the fleet appeared to combine elements of both direct and cross-trade. The sub-

Table 4.1
Soviet Vessel Deployment by Trade Type during 1983
(trading non-tanker vessels over 3,000 tonnes)

Trade type	Number of vessels	%
Direct trade	601	46
Combined direct and cross-trade	358	28
Cross-trade	32	2
Insufficient data	306	24
Total	1,297	100

stantial 'insufficient data' category suggests that a large number of vessels were engaged for long periods in Soviet internal trade, thus escaping the Lloyd's net.

There are variations in the above proportions for different types of vessel. The types of vessel unlikely to be a challenge to Western shipping include bulkers, ore carriers and various miscellaneous trading types such as refrigerated ships and cargo/training vessels. Although it might be expected that these would be mainly operating in direct trades a quarter of this small category of vessel types appears to combine cross-trading and direct trade. This is because much of bulk trading is essentially one way and cross-trading is an alternative to having a ballast leg to the return journey. However, the total number of vessels involved in this combined trading is relatively small.

General cargo, container and Ro-Ro ships are likely to

Table 4.2
Deployment of Bulk and Ore Carriers and Miscellaneous Trading Vessels during 1983

Trade type	Bulk/ore		Miscellaneous	
	No.	%	No.	%
Direct trade	79	57	14	31
Combined direct and cross-trade	33	24	20	44
Cross-trade	4	3	1	3
Insufficient data	23	16	10	22
Total	139	100	45	100

concern the Western shipowner more than bulkers and most of the vessels analysed are of this type. It appears that a very small proportion of conventional general cargo ships are engaged purely in cross-trading though the proportion is higher among unitized vessels (Table 4.3). This analysis shows that the Soviet fleet is substantially engaged in carrying cargo between the Soviet Union and other countries. One fact which becomes clear is that trade with associated states keeps large numbers of vessels busy. In total 1,013 general cargo vessels were monitored; 163, or 16 per cent of them spent at least part of the year on the route between Cuba and the Soviet Union. Although this figure is notable other countries appear to have less significant links. Few general cargo vessels were on the Vietnam route, 28 were linked with Angola and 18 with Mozambique. In total this means that 20 per cent of the general cargo fleet is to some extent engaged in trade unlikely to be available to Western shipping lines.

The number of vessels which never enter deep-sea international trade is even more striking. As many as 320 of the 1,013 general cargo vessels monitored remained in North Europe, the Black Sea and the Mediterranean for the whole of 1983. Fifty-one ships did not go further than the Red Sea and Gulf of Aden. These figures are very high considering that small vessels were excluded from the analysis. While it would be expected that small ships would have rather restricted itineraries it is surprising that so many larger ones do not venture far from home. The importance of trade with the European and Mediterranean neighbours of the Soviet Union mentioned earlier (Tables 2.1 and 2.2) is clear.

4.4 Analysis of modern liner vessels

The Soviet fleet contains few unitized vessels, whether fully cellular, semi-container or Ro-Ro compared with most of the major maritime states. There are no large cellular vessels and only seven of the Ro-Ro ships can carry over a thousand twenty-foot equivalent units (TEU). It is important to examine the activities of the few Soviet container carrying vessels because:

Table 4.3
Deployment of General Cargo and Unitized Vessels during 1983

Trade type	General cargo[1]		Container/Ro-Ro	
	No.	%	No.	%
Direct trade	478	47	30	30
Combined direct and cross-trade	269	27	36	36
Cross-trade	14	1	13	13
Insufficient data	252	25	21	21
Total	1,013	100	100	100

[1] Including semi-container ships.

(1)   these are the best vessels in the fleet and therefore should be deployed on routes considered important;

(2)   these are the vessels most able to compete effectively with Western lines in terms of speed, turnaround time and facilities;

(3)   container vessels can have three to five times the productivity of conventional vessels of the same size, mainly due to much faster cargo handling.

There are four classes of medium to large Soviet Ro-Ros (Table 4.4). The largest vessels, four Magnitogorsks spent the whole of 1983 serving Cuba directly from the Soviet Union. Two Skulptor class vessels were also devoted to this trade and one direct call by an Atlantica class vessel was made. This means that 40,000 TEU slots of the best quality the fleet could provide were dedicated to Soviet direct trade with Cuba during the year. The next largest vessels are in the Atlantica class (1,200 TEU). These were deployed on a combined direct

Table 4.4
Large and Medium-Sized Soviet Ro-Ros, 1984

Class	Number of vessels	dwt	TEU capacity
Magnitogorsk	4	21,002	1,368
Atlantica	3	20,175	1,200
Skulptor	6	18,462	772
Petr Masherov	2	18,000	634

and cross-trade service sailing from a Soviet Black Sea port to Vietnam with Soviet exports, then sailing to Japan and returning to the Black Sea via Mersin in the Eastern Mediterranean. It is presumed that cross-trade cargoes were carried on the Japan–Mersin leg although the volume of trade could not be very large. Five of the remaining vessels (Skulptor and Petr Masherov classes) were on the trade between the Baltic/North Europe and Australia/New Zealand. The Soviet Baltic Shipping Company is a member of the New Zealand European Shipping Association and the Australia to Europe Shipping Conference. The sixth Skulptor was not on a set route but engaged in direct sailings from the Soviet Union to Cuba, Vietnam and Angola. In summary then, the best Soviet Ro-Ros are primarily used to trade with Soviet partners or are operating within a major freight conference.

There are three classes of medium-sized fully cellular vessels (Table 4.5). The largest currently operating are the Kapitan class at 932 TEU, and under twenty thousand gross tons. This is no more than medium-sized by world standards; there are 375 larger container ships in the world, many carrying over 2,000 TEU and some carrying 4,000 TEU. During 1983 all Kapitan class vessels, plus seven of the 824 TEU Mercur class were deployed on the North Europe–South-East Asia cross-trade providing weekly sailings on the route. Occasional diversions to Leningrad were made. The three remaining Mercur vessels plus one of the Pula class were engaged in cross-trading between the Far East and Australia although numerous direct calls in the Soviet Far East were made. Three remaining Pula class vessels were devoted to the short hop between Japanese ports and Nakhodka or Vostochny

Table 4.5
Medium-Sized Fully Cellular Soviet Vessels, 1984

Class	Number of vessels	dwt	TEU capacity
Kapitan	4*	15,950	932
Mercur/Khudozhnik	10	14,490	824
Pula conversions	4	14,170	700

* Only 3 had been delivered by 1983.

in the Soviet Far East. Although this is apparently a direct trade route it is believed that the vessels are transit cargo feeders for the Trans-Siberian Container Service. The activities of the largest fully-cellular Soviet ships can therefore be summarized as being almost wholly devoted to cross-trading.

Since there are so few medium-sized or large container carrying vessels in the Soviet fleet it may also be useful to examine the trading patterns of smaller vessels. There are numerous Ro-Ros, cellular ships and semi-container vessels with capacities of 200 to 400 TEU deployed on a wide variety of trades (Table 4.6). In addition there are numerous general cargo vessels with some sort of container carrying capability though generally not exceeding 200 TEU. The eighteen ships of the Leninskaya Gvardiya class and the twenty-strong Pioner Moskvy class are typical. Some bulk carriers have also been seen carrying containers, notably the Kapitan Khromtsov class. This further analysis concentrates on 65 smaller vessels appearing in the ship movements data and primarily engaged in container carrying work. A notable characteristic of this group was the frequent switching of vessels from one trade route to another. Shipowners in the West generally keep the same vessels on the same routes for long periods, in some

Table 4.6
Some Classes of Smaller Soviet Container Carrying Vessels

Class	Number of vessels	dwt	TEU capacity
Roll-on, roll-off			
Hamlet Multiflex	2	12,600	380
Kapitan Tomson	2	7,240	333
Neva	9	4,600	292
Inzhenier Machulskiy	9	6,128	250
Akademik	6	4,267	235
Fully cellular			
Aleksandr Fadeyev	5	6,494	358
Sestroretsk	6	6,270	218
Semi-container			
Dnepr	12	13,500	388
Warnemunde	17	12,347	368

cases for the full life of the ship. In contrast Morflot vessels of this size appear to be treated as forming a general pool. Liner services are maintained by taking a variety of vessels from the pool and deploying them on routes for only one or two round voyages before replacing them with other vessels from the pool.

As with the large Ro-Ros, numerous smaller container carrying vessels are engaged solely in carrying the exports and imports of the Soviet Union. In fact 39 per cent of the movements of these smaller vessels were found to be wholly committed to direct trades particularly within North Europe and the Mediterranean. A somewhat higher proportion of movements, 46 per cent, was of vessels combining direct and cross-trading activity in various parts of the world. Although there is a cross-trading element in the schedules of over half of the smaller container ships none are purely cross-trading and the capacity available for cross-trade cargoes on any single route is not great. The busiest route, Black Sea–Mediterranean–Red Sea, has the equivalent of only five and a half vessels of around 300 TEU capacity allocated to it to carry both direct and cross-traded cargoes. Substantial gaps in the schedules of ships analysed, possibly explained by intra-USSR trading represented about 13 per cent of movements. Additionally there is a little confused scheduling from which a trade route could not be identified. None of the 65 small container ships has a purely cross-trade based schedule.

4.5   Pattern of cross-trading

Our analysis of Soviet ship schedules provides evidence that very few vessels are employed purely in cross-trading. The tonnage devoted to this activity is probably smaller for the Soviet Union than for most other major maritime powers. However, a substantial volume of tonnage combines cross-trading with direct trades. It would appear that many Soviet vessels leaving Baltic ports load additional cargo in North Europe before sailing to a destination. Similarly ships departing from Soviet Black Sea ports often call in the Mediterranean, though more often in the Eastern Mediterranean than say Italy or France where more substantial volumes may be available. In returning to the Black and Baltic Seas similar cross-trading calls are commonly made. This suggests that cross-trade cargoes are being used to 'top up'. There is little evidence to suggest that cross-trading is a device to carry cargo on what would otherwise be a ballast leg except with some bulk/ore carriers. Where European calls are made they normally occur on both outward and homeward legs of a round voyage. A possible exception is the Ro-Ro service on the route Black Sea–Vietnam–Japan–Eastern Mediterranean– Black Sea. Here Soviet exports move to Vietnam and the vessels sail lightly loaded to Japan to pick up cargo bound for the Eastern Mediterranean. But even in this case the import of heavy construction equipment from Japan to the Black Sea goes some way to explain the schedule.

The analysis also reveals that Cuba and other political allies have substantial volumes of quality tonnage assigned to them thus limiting the vessels available to compete with the West. Short-sea shipping within Europe and the Mediterranean also accounts for much of the activity of the general cargo fleet. Many of the large Ro-Ros are devoted to Soviet bilateral trades. By contrast the larger fully cellular container ships are mainly involved in cross-trading. The many smaller container carrying vessels are on direct trades but with a cross-trading element in nearly half of the cases examined.

Finally, it is clear that few Soviet vessels remain on fixed routes for long periods. Only a small number of general cargo vessels were assigned to a set route for the whole of 1983. In the West, by contrast, a ship can remain on the same liner route for all or most of its life. This switching of vessels and the introduction of irregular deviations/calls may explain the poor service quality, which is a feature of Soviet liner operations (Chapter 5).

CHAPTER FIVE

Soviet Competition in the Liner Market

5.1 Liner conferences and Soviet shipping

The most controversial aspect of the Soviet shipping is that
of competition in the liner market. This chapter begins by
examining the nature of the liner shipping industry and the
criticisms levelled at Soviet participants. There then follows a
detailed examination of Soviet involvement on each of the
major trade routes followed by an assessment of the impact of
such competition.

A liner shipping service is one which provides regular,
scheduled sailings from one or a range of ports to another port
or range. Single shipments take up a small part of vessel
capacity and the consignments of many shippers are carried
in a single voyage. Liner cargo is dominated by manufactured
goods, higher value foodstuffs and semi-bulk commodities. Liner services in most parts of the world are dominated
by the so-called freight conferences. These are groupings of
shipping lines serving particular routes or geographical areas.
Many conferences agree the capacity to be offered by each
company and all establish a freight rate structure, often
complex, which conference members are expected to enforce.
In short, to the extent that shipping conferences control both
capacity and price they operate as cartels.

On some routes, freight conference cartels have often
controlled total supply of liner shipping. The main competi-

tion faced by these cartels has, in the past, been with the tramp sector at the bottom end of the market (low value goods) and with airfreighting at the top end (high value goods). Most of the main liner conferences have also faced significant levels of 'outsider' competition from other liner firms which are not members of the conference. If conference action through competitive pricing or maintaining customer loyalty succeeds, the outsider may withdraw from the route. In numerous cases, the outsider becomes established and eventually joins the conference, or he may become a 'tolerated outsider'. Nowadays, one of the most serious problems for conference members is the existence of established non-conference firms, many with large-scale container shipping operations. In some cases it would appear that they have not been permitted to join the conference, in others they seem content to remain outside. Often the problem is one of agreeing on trade shares as outsiders negotiating conference membership are likely to be offered a smaller share of the trade than they already carry.

Soviet lines are members of a few conferences and are non-conference competitors on numerous other routes (Table 5.1). Where they are members their loading rights are, in several cases, restricted to Soviet or Eastern European ports. Such cases are discussed in detail below.

Table 5.1
Soviet Freight Conference Membership

Company	Conference
Baltic Shipping Co.	Brazil/Europe/Brazil Freight Conference
	Europe Argentina Freight Conference
	Argentina Europe Freight Conference
	New Zealand European Shipping Association
	Australia to Europe Shipping Conference
	Continent to Australia Conference
Estonian Shipping Co.	Continent West Africa Conf. (COWAC)
Black Sea Shipping Co.	Member of eighteen of the conferences under the umbrella of India–Pakistan–Bangladesh Conferences
Latvian Shipping Co.	The Levant Conference

Source: Croner's *World Directory of Freight Conferences*.

5.2 Soviet rate-cutting

It is when considering liner markets where Soviet lines compete as outsiders that criticism of Soviet shipping operations has been most vociferous. It stems from the belief that Soviet liner firms are consistently and systematically undercutting conference freight rates thereby undermining the commercial viability of all liner operators in those markets. There is some difficulty in establishing direct first-hand evidence of Soviet undercutting of liner freight rates. However, several shipping authorities with direct involvement in particular trades have collected such evidence. As early as 1977, B. Heldring of the Royal Netherlands Steamship Company (KNSM Group NV) claimed that Soviet underquotations for certain commodities between Europe and South or Central America had been as follows:

3,100 tonnes cotton	: 45 per cent	
3,500 tonnes coffee	: 37 per cent	
1,300 tonnes butter milk	: 34 per cent	below conference rate
7,000 tonnes chemicals	: 30 per cent	
6,000 tonnes milk powder	: 27 per cent	
3,000 tonnes steel	: 25 per cent	

Heldring argued that the conference members concerned had either had to match these quotations or give up the cargoes (Heldring, 1977).

The liner routes on which Soviet outsiders have faced most criticism have been those between Europe and the Far East. A 1984 confidential study by the General Council of British Shipping (GCBS) found that on UK – Far East services Soviet rates were generally 18 to 30 per cent below those charged by conference members. In the period September to November 1984 on westbound services Soviet quotations were found to be 14 to 34 per cent below conference rates on a range of twenty commodities including textiles, plastic goods, toys and audio/video equipment. Eastbound Soviet rates on a range of thirty commodities, including household removals, machinery and car parts, were 10 to 52 per cent lower. In most cases Soviet rates were claimed to be lower than those of the two largest outsiders namely Evergreen and Yang Ming, both

Taiwanese operators. The GCBS also claim to have evidence of underquotations for Soviet vessels returning to Europe from Mozambique and picking up cargoes in East Africa.

More recent rates information has been supplied for the present study from sources associated with Far East liner services in Rotterdam. A small number of examples may give some impression of the sort of differential between conference rates and Soviet outsiders in mid-1985. A significant European export cargo to South-East Asia is milk powder. The fully inclusive rate charged in 1985 by a conference line (after currency and bunker adjustment factors, contractor's discount and forwarder's commission at mid-1985 values) from the Continent to Singapore or Hong Kong would have been US $1,072 to $1,150. This compares with a Balt Orient rate of $985 to $1,050. For this particular commodity the Soviet line was undercutting by only around 8 per cent. However, a similar comparison can be made for machinery exports from the Continent to Singapore. For a particular shipment a freight conference quote of $2,172, fully inclusive, would have applied. Balt Orient would have charged $1,278; undercutting by 41 per cent. Between these extremes a third example is for vehicle parts exported from Europe to the Continent. A conference rate of $1,563 compared with $1,278 for Balt Orient. The outsider was undercutting by 18 per cent in this example. All three were rates for one twenty-foot container.

Such results must be treated with caution as much depends on such factors as the level of forwarding agents' commission, rebates, the payload for the equipment and the degree of flexibility concerning the conference rate. The example of machinery to Singapore may, if the shipment was considered attractive, have been subjected to a 'Special Cargo Quote' offering perhaps 15 to 25 per cent off. This would have reduced the conference rate to between $1,846 and $1,629. Furthermore, the Far East Freight Conference now has an 'action unit' which can authorize combative freight rates to win shipments from outsiders and this has great flexibility over pricing.

There is little doubt that Soviet undercutting takes place on many routes where Soviet lines operate as outsiders. However, they are not the only outsiders undercutting conference rates nor are they always the worst. It is commonplace for outsiders competing with conference members in any particular trade to undercut conference rates by around 10 per cent. This in practice means 10 per cent below the discounted conference rates though on occasions the outsider may go down as far as 20 per cent or more.

The criticism levelled at Soviet liner operations has been much more wide-ranging than that of rate-cutting as the following lengthy quotation shows:

> The trade from East Africa to Europe for some time has been under severe attack from Russian competition, and it has been specifically known from the sighting of instructions from Leningrad to agents that the latter were authorised to quote as much as 25 per cent under Conference rates without reference and higher margins on quick reference back for authority. The reason for the drive for northbound cargo was that Russian ships were carrying supplies to Mozambique mostly of a military nature, particularly at the time of the guerilla warfare in Zimbabwe. It was natural that the Russians should seek cargoes at any price level. This would earn some foreign exchange and make a marginal contribution to the cost of what would otherwise be a homeward ballast voyage resulting from an outward voyage justified by strategic consideration . . .
>
> They are at present undercutting rates of freight very substantially in the trade between Europe, the Red Sea and South East Asia, exacerbating price competition which exists in any case in these trades. Previously they were a force for instability in the Atlantic and Pacific trades.
>
> For some time they have undermined prices in various Central American trades and trades with East and West Africa. If Morflot had been a private enterprise company it would have been in liquidation long ago, and traders who had relied on it would have suddenly found themselves lacking the services they depended on. If they had been owned by almost any state in the Western world there would by now have been a public outcry on the scale of losses assuming their accounts had been cast in Western terms. (Swayne, 1983)

To assess the validity of such accusations a closer examination of the main liner trade routes on which Soviet competition exists is necessary. The best documented example is the North Atlantic in the 1970s. This is examined below. Later sections contain detailed analyses of the nature and quality of Soviet competition on liner routes where Soviet lines operate as conference members as well as on routes where they are outsiders.

5.3   Soviet liner competition on the North Atlantic

The most concentrated and best documented cross-trading activity by Soviet lines was found on the routes from North Europe to North America during the 1970s. Concern at the growth and activities of Soviet lines was voiced in the United States during the period and investigations by bodies including the Department of Commerce followed. As a result, a certain amount of reliable data on freight rates and market penetration is available. This makes a brief analysis of the market worthwhile despite the fact that the service is now much depleted.

Until 1971 the International Longshoremen's Association had, for over twenty years, refused to handle Soviet cargo. The relaxation of the ban enabled Soviet firms rapidly to develop cross-trading lines on various routes but predominantly from the US East Coast to the UK, North Continent and Scandinavia (Table 5.2). By the second half of the 1970s, many of the best

Table 5.2
USSR Liner Fleet Penetration of Trade Routes between US North Atlantic Ports and North Europe

Year	Tonnes carried	%
1974	328,900	4.2
1975	270,900	4.5
1976	320,900	4.9
1977	308,900	5.3
1978 (9 months)	266,600	5.3

Source: Marad, US Department of Commerce.

unitized Soviet vessels were on this trade including the large Ro-Ros and the Mercur class containerships. Four North Atlantic liner services existed: Balt Atlantic and Balt Atlantic Ro-Ro, Balt Gulf and Balt Gulf Ro-Ro. Despite the obvious attempts by Soviet lines to build up substantial shares in these trades their success was not great. Except in the major trade between the United States and West Germany where they carried up to 13 per cent of cargo by volume, Soviet participation in individual trade links did not normally exceed 5 per cent in tonnage terms and on the North Atlantic as a whole around 5 per cent was achieved (Department of Trade, 1979). Their performance was thought to have been restricted by a combination of poor service, lack of market intelligence and conference loyalty on the part of many shippers.

For long periods in the 1970s outsider participation on North Atlantic trades was substantial. For example in the first half of 1975 outsiders carried 55 per cent of containerable cargo westbound from the Hamburg–Antwerp range (CENSA, 1976). Soviet activity must be seen within this picture of extensive competitive action by non-conference lines which at the time included CAST and Europe Canada Lakes Line. Studies by the US government showed that Balt America charged the lowest rates, on average, in half of the North Atlantic trades. This means, of course, that non-Soviet out-

Table 5.3
Level of Soviet Undercutting in US Trades, 1977

	Range of differential		Number of observations
	High %	Low %	
North Atlantic/UK and Eire	18	2	39
North Atlantic/Scandinavia, Baltic	43	4	40
North Atlantic/West Germany	16	3	46
North Atlantic/Netherlands, Belgium	10	1	44
North Atlantic/France, Northern Spain	50	4	41

Note: These figures exclude observations of Soviet rates being higher than the conferences.

Source: US Federal Maritime Commission, Soviet Maritime Activities in Liner Trades of the USA, 1977.

siders charged lower rates on the other half. Furthermore, in some cases the Soviet lines charged higher rates than the conference. Where they did undercut, the level of undercutting was very variable (Table 5.3).

It should be borne in mind that Balt Atlantic made serious efforts to join the North Atlantic Conferences. At one time agreement was reached in principle but this was scuppered, according to the Soviets, because of pressure from Washington (Maslov, 1984). Certainly Soviet lines have preferred wherever possible to be within rather than without the conference. In 1980 as a result of the longshoremen's boycott in the United States, Balt Atlantic discontinued its services. This did not stop the downward pressure on rates in the North Atlantic trades. Rates continued to decline for some time because of general overtonnaging both by conference members and outsiders. This in itself shows that Soviet undercutting was perhaps a symptom of rather than the basic cause of instability. Widespread overtonnaging was the real problem yet Soviet market penetration was only 4 to 5 per cent.

5.4   The competitive posture of Soviet liner services

The competitive impact of Soviet shipping companies in the liner trades, whether they are conference members or outsiders, depends partly on their freight rates but also on the quality of the liner services they provide. The quality of such services depends on their frequency and regularity, the total capacity offered, the speed and reliability of sailings and the type of vessels and facilities available. Small, slow general cargo vessels with poor reliability and limited handling facilities will clearly be less competitive than fast modern container vessels offering substantial capacity. Service quality must always be measured against the competition on a given route since what is acceptable to shippers in, say, Mozambique may not be acceptable in Japan or Germany. A service which runs on average two days behind schedule may be the best available on one route and the poorest on another.

Soviet lines' tariff policies and the criticism made of them have been discussed earlier. Critics of Soviet liner operations have, however, consistently ignored the quality of service element. The analysis which follows sets out to put this right by analysing in detail the major Soviet liner services out of Europe. Where possible, key service features of each Soviet line are examined but in presenting the results it has not been possible to keep a consistent format because of differing data sources.

The transit times and reliability analysis is based on Lloyd's data as presented in Lloyd's Export Shipping magazine, which ceased publication during 1985. The periods analysed vary for the different routes but are all in the 1980s and are of nine or twelve months' duration. The transit times tables show the time in days for a ship to travel from one port to another. Averages for all the sailings tracked for the Soviet lines are compared with those for the fastest and slowest lines operating between the ports under consideration. The tables also show the ranking of the Soviet line in order of speed of transit between the ports.

As a measure of reliability actual vessel departure dates are compared with those advertised by each line. The last loading port in North-West Europe or Scandinavia is taken as a reference point. Departure dates extracted from schedules published eighteen or nineteen days ahead of a planned sailing are compared with actual performance to indicate how far vessels slip behind during loading cycles. The figures are for average days off schedule for the sailings of each line checked. Capacity shares have been calculated for some routes, either in TEU or tonnage terms. These do not appear on routes where some lines devote only part of their capacity to the destinations being considered.

5.5 Soviet liner services operating within conferences

5.5.1 Balt America

This service from North Europe to South American East Coast is operated jointly by the Baltic Shipping Corporation of the USSR; Polish Ocean Lines; and, VEB, Deutfracht/Seereederei, of Rostok, East Germany. The joint service is operating within the Argentina and Brazil conferences.

61

Table 5.4
Average Transit Times on Conventional Services – North Europe
to East Coast of South America (October 1982–September 1983)

Santos from Hamburg – ranking 1st of 11 lines

Balt America	20.6 days
slowest	31.5 days

Santos from Rotterdam – ranking 3rd of 12 lines

fastest	19.1 days
Balt America	21.5 days
slowest	36.8 days

Rio from Hamburg – ranking 1st of 9 lines

Balt America	18.2 days
slowest	32.0 days

Buenos Aires from Rotterdam – ranking 6th of 11 lines

fastest	28.2 days
Balt America	30.5 days
slowest	50.8 days

Buenos Aires from Antwerp – ranking 6th of 11 lines

fastest	19.3 days
Balt America	28.2 days
slowest	46.9 days

Note: Rankings in this and subsequent tables refer to the ranking of Soviet
liner companies in terms of average transit times.

The service employs various conventional vessels in the
8,000 to 13,000 dwt range and semi-containership of the
Palekh class (368 TEU). Vessels call at Baltic ports then
Hamburg/Rotterdam/Antwerp. Hamburg is served with 10-
day frequency; the others, every three weeks. The usual South
American calls are: Rio de Janeiro, Santos, Montevideo,
Buenos Aires, Puerto Madryn.

Analysis of transit times (Table 5.4) shows that the Soviet
service is among the fastest available to the East Coast of
South America (ECSA) from North Europe as far as conventional services are concerned. However, four operators are
now providing separate fast container services not included
in this analysis. Combined figures for container and conventional services would give the Soviets above average transit
times.

Of the 25 conventional services identified the Soviets come
top on grounds of reliability, averaging only 2.15 days off

schedule. Of the unitized operators only ELMA beats this, being 1.00 days off. On this route a fairly low service quality tends to be the norm. Cargo volumes are small; the services are predominantly conventional. The Soviet service is provided primarily to serve the Eastern Bloc but capacity remains for cargo from the North Continent. As conference members the Russians cannot compete in terms of price as there is a conference tariff but appear to be able to compete successfully in terms of service quality, offering a relatively fast, very reliable service with some container capacity. There is no indication of their presence causing instability or excessive over-capacity.

The Soviets operate as members of the Europe Argentina Freight Conference, Argentina Europe Freight Conference, Brazil/Europe/Brazil Freight Conference. Each of these divides the European end into areas and members have loading rights pertaining to these. The Baltic Shipping Corporation (BSC) has substantial rights in the Baltic areas and rights limited by agreement with conference colleagues in the Hamburg-Bordeaux range. It has no loading rights in the British Isles. As the participation levels show (Table 5.5) this arrangement enables the BSC to provide 9 per cent of annual capacity on the route. They are the only conference cross-trader as far as North Europe is concerned.

5.5.2 Blasco Indostan

Blasco Indostan is a conventional and Ro-Ro service operating within the UK and Continent – India, Pakistan and Bangladesh Conferences. It is operated by the Black Sea Shipping Corporation and provides approximately one sailing every three weeks, the usual itinerary being:

Portbury	Karachi
Rotterdam	Bombay
Antwerp (occasional calls)	Calcutta
Bremen	Madras
Hamburg	Cochin (Chittagong).

Vessels employed include 380 TEU Ro-Ros of the Izvestiya class and 7,700 tonnes deadweight conventional liners such as

Table 5.5
Annual Capacity Shares among the Brazil/Europe/Brazil and Europe
Argentina Freight Conference Lines and Competitors 1982–3

Lines	NRT/ annum	% conference	% total trade
South American			
Alianca (Brazil)	334,690	14	
ELMA (Argentina)	320,610	14	
Lloyd Brazileiro (Brazil)	266,860	12	
Ciamar (Argentina)	112,380	5	
Sub-total	1,034,540	45	43
North European			
DFDS/Effoa (Denmark)	47,770	2	
BHLR (UK)	151,500	7	
Josal (Sweden)	82,110	4	
Hamburg Sud (Germany)	416,690	18	
SEAS (France)	102,250	4	
Havenlijn (Netherlands)	67,160	3	
Nedlloyd (Netherlands)	90,000	4	
RSAL (Netherlands)	100,170	4	
Sub-total	1,057,650	46	44
Cross-Trader			
Balt America (USSR)	215,060	9	9
Conference total	2,307,250	100	
Outsider			
Eurosudam (Germany)	102,000		4
Trade total	2,409,250		100

Mikhail Stenko. All are owned by the Black Sea Shipping Company and were built between 1972 and 1979.

Blasco's transit times tend to be above average on a route which generally has a fairly poor standard of service. Between some ports, such as Bombay and Hamburg, Blasco is on average the fastest operator (Table 5.6).

Of the ten conventional services on this route the Soviet line is ranked fourth in terms of reliability. At ten days off schedule it falls in a range of four to thirty-two days off. It should be noted that there are also ten unitized operators on the route, most of whom possess greater reliability than the

Table 5.6
Average Transit Times for Conventional Services on the North
Europe to India/Pakistan/Bangladesh Trades
(August 1981–July 1982)

Bombay from Hamburg – ranked 1st of 8 lines	
fastest (Blasco Indostan)	35.3 days
slowest	53.6 days
Karachi from Bremen – ranked 3rd of 7 lines	
fastest	28.3 days
Blasco Indostan	33.3 days
slowest	55.2 days
Karachi from UK ports – ranked 3rd of 6 lines	
fastest	27.3 days
Blasco Indostan	32.3 days
slowest	67.6 days
Madras from Rotterdam – ranked 2nd of 5 lines	
fastest	40.9 days
Blasco Indostan	47.8 days
slowest	65.2 days

Note: Rankings are those of Blasco Indostan.

Soviet service. Overall Blasco Indostan provides only 7 per cent of conference capacity on a route dominated by Southern Asian lines. Capacity is calculated from the round trips by each vessel and its net registered tonnage (Table 5.7).

5.5.3 United West Africa Service (UWAS)

UWAS is a joint Soviet/Polish/East German service from Continent to West Africa within the Continent West Africa Conference. The lines involved are the Estonian Shipping Company, Tallinn; Polish Ocean Lines, Gdynia; and VEB Deutfracht/Seereederei, Rostock. UWAS used to operate two distinct European loading rotations – from the Hamburg/ Antwerp range and from northern France. During the year under review, (December 1982 to end November 1983) there was a degree of overlap between the two. Ports served are Hamburg, Rotterdam, Antwerp, Dunkirk and Rouen and vessels calling at German and Benelux ports may also make a French call. From Germany and Benelux, the usual West African rotation is Banjul, Freetown, Monrovia, Tema. Dakar,

Table 5.7
Annual Capacity Shares in the UK and Continent/India, Pakistan,
Bangladesh Freight Conferences (1981–2)

	% total annual capacity	
European Lines		
Anchor Line (UK)	6	
Compagnie Générale Maritime (France)	6	
COBRA (International consortium)	10	
Sub-total		22
Southern Asia Lines		
Bangladesh Shipping Corporation (Bangladesh)	5	
India Steamship Co. (India)	9	
Parkistan National Shipping Corporation (Pakistan)	12	
Scindia (India)	14	
Shipping Corporation of India (India)	17	
Sub-total		57
Cross-traders		
Blasco Indostan (USSR)	7	
Deutfracht Seereederei, Rostok (E. Germany)	2	
Polish Ocean Lines (Poland)	12	
Sub-total		21
Total		100

Abidjan, Lome, Lagos/Apapa, Douala, Owendo/Libreville and Pointe Noire are also served. Less frequent calls were reported from Takoradi, Calabar, Cotonou, Port Harcourt, Conakry, Kribi and Sao Tome. Principal ports served on the French operation were Banjul and Abidjan. Less frequent calls were reported from a number of ports in the Dakar/Luanda range.

Up to four sailings per month are offered from the Hamburg/Antwerp range, averaging three per month. There are two to three sailings monthly on average from French ports. Frequencies between individual ports are lower. Vessels used are drawn from a pool maintained by member lines. Ships range in age from late 1950s built tonnage to early 1970s and in size from 4,200 dwt to 10,000 dwt. Some heavy-lift, reefer, liquids and container capacity is available.

In an analysis of the reliability of advertised schedules, UWAS is fairly average being ranked sixteenth of 37 operators. However, all the first twenty lines were less than six days off schedule. On the other hand, Soviet transit times to some of the most frequently served ports such as Freetown and Tema are poor but they do well in competition with some of the smaller operators to small ports such as Banjul (Table 5.8). All the data presented here refer to the service calling at the Hamburg/Antwerp range. Lack of information prevented inclusion of the UWAS service from French ports.

5.5.4 Balt Australia

Balt Australia operates as a member of the Continent Australia Conference from Eastern Europe, Scandinavia and the Mediterranean to Australia. It was an outsider to New Zealand but in 1985 it also became a member of the relevant conference. For northbound services it is within the conferences from both Australia and New Zealand. The line is operated by the Baltic Shipping Company of Leningrad. Five Skulptor class Ro-Ros are employed on the trade. Built between 1976 and 1982 they are normally about 18,000 dwt,

Table 5.8
Average Transit Times on the Continent – West Africa Trade
(December 1982 to November 1983)

Freetown from Hamburg – ranking 4th of 5 lines	
fastest	16.8 days
UWAS	23.7 days
slowest	24.0 days
Tema from Hamburg – ranking 5th of 6 lines	
fastest	17.7 days
UWAS	27.8 days
slowest	30.7 days
Tema from Rotterdam – ranking 6th of 6 lines	
fastest	15.6 days
UWAS	28.9 days
Banjul from Antwerp – ranking 1st of 2 lines	
UWAS	12.3 days
slowest	20.0 days

carrying 634 TEU and offering 80 reefer slots. All the other major lines on this route use container vessels of 1,000 to 2,000 TEU. This enables Balt Australia to offer conventional, container and Ro-Ro space on a monthly basis with the following schedule:

Leningrad	Freemantle
Kotka/Helsinki	Adelaide
Rostok	Melbourne
Bilbao	Sydney
Barcelona	Auckland
Marseilles	Napier
Genoa	Lyttelton
	Bluff Harbour

Balt Australia competes with one other direct Scandinavian caller, Scan Carriers, and is the only line calling at a Finnish port direct. Most Scandinavian cargo is transhipped on the North Continent. As a result the transit times analysis (Table 5.9) is limited, but it does show that Balt Australia is much slower than its major competitor Scan Carriers normally taking at least one week longer. There was insufficient scheduling data to monitor the reliability of the Balt Australia service.

Table 5.9
Transit Times on the Scandinavia–Australasia Trade
(June 1983 to April 1984)

Sydney from Scandinavia – ranking 3rd out of 3 lines	
Scan Carriers (Schedule A)	42.4 days
(Schedule B)	37.1 days
Balt Australia	49.4 days
Auckland from Scandinavia – ranking 2nd out of 2 lines	
Scan Carriers	44.9 days
Balt Australia	57.0 days

5.6 Soviet liner services operated as outsiders

5.6.1 Balt Orient

The Baltic Shipping Corporation operates one of the most

successful Soviet liner operations, the Balt Orient Line. The services cover North Europe to South-East Asia, also calling at Jeddah with approximately weekly sailings of fully cellular vessels. This service was previously under the name Odessa Ocean Line and was operated by the Black Sea Shipping Corporation. Vessels of 732 to 932 TEU are now employed. The largest and most modern fully cellular vessels in the Soviet fleet are dedicated to this service including the 932 TEU Kapitan Gavrilov class and the 732 to 824 TEU Khudozhnik class. These are competing with some of the largest container ships afloat carrying 2,000 to 3,000 TEU and owned by major consortia.

There are two roughly alternating itineraries:

1. Hamburg	2. Hamburg
Bremerhaven	Gothenburg
Rotterdam	
Antwerp	Rotterdam
Tilbury	Tilbury
Le Havre	Le Havre
Jeddah	Jeddah
Singapore	
Manila	Singapore
Hong Kong	Hong Kong
Port Kelang	Penang

These differ from the itineraries of most other operators on the route who incorporate Japanese, Taiwanese and Korean ports in their Far East – Europe services.

An analysis of transit times shows that the Balt Orient service is slowest of all operators on some ports of the route and one of the slowest to other ports (Table 5.10). At the same time, of the eight unitized operations on the Far East route Balt Orient was the least reliable (Table 5.11). It should be added, however, that the standard of service on the trade is particularly high. Of 13 Balt Orient schedules checked the average delay was 2.15 days. This was the worst of the eight operators even though most of the others had many more sailings. All but one of the other operators were less than a day off schedule.

Balt Orient only accounts for 4 per cent of capacity on the route, which is dominated by large consortia. Another out-

Table 5.10
Transit Times on the North Europe–South-East Asia Trade
(June 1983 to May 1984)

Hong Kong from Hamburg – ranking 8th out of 9 lines
        fastest   21.0 days
        Balt Orient   34.6 days
        slowest   36.3·days
        (based on 42 Balt Orient sailings monitored)

Hong Kong from Le Havre – ranking 7th out of 7 lines
        fastest   24.0 days
        slowest (Balt Orient)   27.8 days
        (based on 41 Balt Orient sailings monitored)

Singapore from UK – ranking 4th out of 6 lines
        fastest   19.0 days
        Balt Orient   23.0 days
        slowest   26.3 days
        (based on 45 Balt Orient sailings)

Table 5.11
Reliability of Liner Schedules

Unitized operators North Europe to Far East excluding
China and Indonesia: 1 June 1983 to 31 May 1984

Rank	Line	Sailings identified	Schedules checked	Days off maximum	Schedule average
1	Maersk	27	27	1	0.07
2	ScanDutch	53	44	1	0.09
3	Trio B (Japan and Korea)	58	58	4	0.24
4	Trio A (South East Asia)	47	45	3	0.33
5	Evergreen	33	10	2	0.70
6	Ace	53	48	5	0.77
7	Yang Ming	22	16	4	1.38
8	Balt Orient	49	13	4	2.15

Source: Lloyd's *Export Shipping*, vol. 3, no. 1 (1984).

sider, Evergreen, has around 10 per cent of capacity (Table 5.12). However, the Trans-Siberian Container Service which operates mainly from Japanese ports is a significant competitor for the conference (see Section 5.9).

Table 5.12
North Europe–Far East Trade 1984 TEU
Capacity Shares on an Annual Basis

	Annual TEU	Capacity %
Conference lines and consortia		
Ace Group (international consortium)	128,676	
DSR (East Germany)	5,232	
Maersk Line (Denmark)	57,200	
Polish Ocean Line (Poland)	8,359	
ScanDutch/MISC (international consortium)	140,946	
Trio (UK, Germany, Japan)	287,315	
Unithai (Thailand)	8,784	
Conference total	636,512	66
Non-conference lines – seaborne		
Balt Orient (USSR)	42,640	(4)
China Ocean Shipping Co. (China)	30,805	
Evergreen (Taiwan)	99,572	
Yang Ming (Taiwan)	38,502	
Non-conference total	211,519	22
*Trans-Siberian Container Service**	122,000	12
Total capacity	970,031	100

* Estimate of maximum annual liftings, westbound.

5.6.2 Balt Orient (Jeddah)

The Saudi Arabian port of Jeddah on the Red Sea is served by a
number of lines on the route from Europe. Some lines offer a
dedicated Red Sea/Arabian Gulf service. Others use Jeddah as
a wayport on a longer route. Balt Orient, along with three
other lines or consortia follow the latter practice and the Soviet
line operates outside the Jeddah Container Rate Agreement.
(Details of the line appear in Section 5.6.1 above.)

Of the four wayport container carriers Balt Orient was
ranked fourth in terms of reliability but all services were of a
high standard. The range was 0.04 to 1.71 days off schedule.
The complexity of this route makes a capacity analysis
meaningless as the wayport carriers will have limited space
allocated to Jeddah. Balt Orient's performance in terms of
comparative transit times appears average (Table 5.13).

71

Table 5.13
Transit Times on the North Europe–Jeddah Trade
(July 1983 to June 1984)

Jeddah from Hamburg – ranking 6th of 12 lines	
fastest	12.6 days
Balt Orient	17.4 days
slowest	18.7 days
Jeddah from Le Havre – ranking 5th of 8 lines	
fastest	10.1 days
Balt Orient	10.7 days
slowest	15.6 days

5.6.3 Besta line

Sailing between Northern Europe and East Africa, Besta is a non-conference operator possibly near to tolerated outsider status. Besta is a conventional and container carrier to Kenya, Tanzania, Mozambique, Madagascar and Mauritius operated by the Baltic Shipping Company. It also competes in the Southern African range with Mozambique calls. Two alternating itineraries are followed:

1.	Leningrad	2.	Leningrad
	Helsingborg		Oskarshamn
	Aarhus		Hamburg
	Hamburg		Rotterdam
	Rotterdam		Antwerp
	Antwerp		London (Northfleet)
	London (Northfleet)		Mombasa
	Mombasa		Dar-es-Salaam
	Dar-es-Salaam		Toamasina
	Nacala (with inducement only)		Mauritius
	Beira		
	Maputo		

Tanga and Zanzibar Island are occasionally served on both rotations and cargo for Zambia is transhipped at Beira. The sailing frequency is fortnightly to Mombasa and Dar-es-Salaam; every four weeks to Beira, Maputo, Toamasina and Mauritius. The vessels employed on the route are taken from a pool of two major classes. There are firstly, the Harry Pollit class of conventional general cargo ships built between 1970

72

and 1972 at 13,150 tonnes deadweight and secondly the Warnemunde class of semi-container ships. The latter were built in the mid-1970s at 11,350 tonnes deadweight. They hold 244 TEU and have capacity for liquid and refrigerated cargo. Eight of the twenty-one vessels in the pool are employed at any one time on this route. In contrast, the main conference lines on the route employ ships built in the 1980s and carrying over 1,000 TEU.

Besta provides an average service to East Africa in terms of reliability, being ranked fourth out of the eight operators and averaging 4.65 days off schedule in a range of 2.28 to 10.60 days off (Table 5.14). Their service to the Indian Ocean Islands is

Table 5.14
Reliability of liner schedules

All operators North Europe to East Africa (Berbera/Nacala range) (December 1982 to November 1983)					
Rank Line	Sailings identified	Schedules checked	Days off Schedule Minimum	Maximum	Average
1 Beacon	18	18	0	10	2.28
2= Baltafrica A	12	9	0	12	3.00
2= Nedlloyd B	5	5	1	7	3.00
4 Besta	26	17	0	17	4.65
5 DOAL	16	13	1	13	5.08
6 Baltafrica B	7	6	4	8	5.17
7 WEC A	11	9	2	16	7.33
8 MSC B	16	10	1	22	10.60

less satisfactory, coming fourth out of five lines. Its Mozambique service, which competes with lines serving Southern Africa, is ranked fifth out of seven lines. Its transit times are around or above average for the route (Table 5.15). Besta is the largest non-conference operator on the route, providing around 15 per cent of capacity (Table 5.16).

5.6.4 Balt Canada and Arctic Line

Arctic Line is part of the Murmansk Shipping Corporation and operates around two sailings per month from North Continent to East Coast Canada often using Strekalovskiy

Table 5.15
Transit Times on the North Europe–East African Trade
(December 1982 to November 1983)

Dar-es-Salaam from UK – ranked 2nd out of 4 lines	
fastest	27.9 days
Besta	29.0 days
Beacon (the major liner consortium)	30.9 days
Mombasa from Hamburg – ranked 1st out of 5 lines	
Besta	27.1 days
slowest	53.3 days
Mombasa from Antwerp – ranked 3rd out of 5 lines	
fastest	19.0 days
Besta	24.2 days
slowest	41.4 days

class bulkers carrying up to 450 TEU. Balt Canada is a separate service provided by the Baltic Shipping Corporation and offers one or two sailings per month using small Ro-Ro vessels carrying up to 292 TEU. The following itineraries are followed:

Balt Canada	Arctic Line
Hamburg	Hamburg
	Bremen
Halifax	Montreal
Montreal (Three Rivers)	Toronto

Most operators serve a much wider range of North American ports and use vessels in the range 1,000 to 2,000 TEU.

Of the twenty-one unitized operators to the East Coast of North America, Balt Canada was the least reliable with the nine sailings checked being three to eleven days behind schedule. Their average was 4.89 days off the advertised time whereas sixteen of the lines were within two days. There was insufficient data during the period of analysis to monitor Arctic Line.

The North Atlantic was faced with severe Soviet competition until 1980 when vessels were banned from their major destination, the United States. Several large Ro-Ros had provided a large service from North Europe (see Section 5.3). Most transatlantic operators still concentrate on US calls. The

Table 5.16
Capacity Shares on North Europe–East Africa Trade

	Aggregate dwt per annum	% share
Conference lines and consortia		
Baltafrica Service A (Poland and East Germany)	152,220	
Baltafrica Service B (Poland and East Germany)	88,795	
Beacon (Consortium)	687,814	
CNN (Portugal)	168,000	
Deutsche Ost-Afrika Linie (Germany)	122,454	
Nedlloyd (Netherlands)	90,000	
Sub-total	1,309,283	67
Non-conference lines		
Besta (USSR)	294,000	(15)
Mediterranean Shipping Co. (Switzerland)	220,548	
West European Container Lines (Netherlands)	134,400	
Sub-total	648,948	33
Total	1,958,231	100

Canadian market is obviously much smaller and Canadian calls for non-Soviet lines are often part of a larger North American service. Thus the Soviet services to Canada operate in competition with lines of the Continental Canadian Westbound Freight Conference and its Eastbound equivalent. Most members are large operators serving the whole of the North American East Coast such as Atlantic Container Line (ACL) and Hapag-Lloyd.

The Soviet services are slow, unreliable, small-scale operations. The few other direct Montreal/Halifax/Toronto calls are part of large, fast, sophisticated services such as SLCS (a joint venture by CP ships, Companie Maritime Belge and Manchester Liners). Soviet transit times are worse than all of these (Table 5.17). The Soviet service is also outclassed by the other Eastern Bloc operator Polish Ocean Lines (POL) which uses modern 1,417 TEU Ro-Ro/cellular vessels and serves a wider range at both ends of the route.

Table 5.17
Transit Times on North Europe to Canada
(October 1982 to September 1983)

Halifax from Hamburg/Bremerhaven – ranking 4th out of 4 lines
        fastest   8.7 days
        Balt Canada (slowest)   10.9 days

Montreal from Hamburg – Balt Canada ranked 2nd out of 3 lines
                         Arctic Line ranked 3rd out of 3 lines
        fastest   13.0 days
        Balt Canada   14.1 days
        Arctic Line (slowest)   15.4 days

There is no evidence that Balt Canada and Arctic Line can compete in terms of frequency, speed or reliability, leaving rates as the key factor. The recent trend has been one of substantial rate increases on the transatlantic. Increases of 12.5 per cent were imposed by the Canadian conferences at the beginning of 1984 and the outsiders followed suit. While Soviet services omit US calls, it is unlikely that they could destabilize what is already a volatile route. Their combined capacity, 1.6 per cent of total on the route is so small as to be insignificant (Table 5.18).

5.7 Soviet liner service operating as a tolerated outsider

5.7.1 Baltcapas

A non-conference liner operator competing with a freight conference may reach a stage where it is well established on a route and appears unlikely to be forced off. A conference may then enter into negotiations with the outside and reach an agreement whereby:

(1) the outsider will not undercut the conference tariff by more than a certain percentage, perhaps 5, 10 or 15 per cent;

Table 5.18
North Europe–North American Eastern Seaboard,
Gulf, St Lawrence and Great Lakes

	TEU capacity shares on an annual basis	
	Estimated annual capacity	% share
Conference lines and consortia		
Sea-Land (US)	221,394	
US Lines (US)	105,668	
Trans Freight Lines (US)	104,755	
Atlantic Container Line (European consortium)	108,000	
St Lawrence Co-ordinated Service (International consortium)	90,748	
Hapag Lloyd (Germany)	89,658	
Cast (Associate members) (Canada)	78,900	
Dart (UK)	53,499	
Atlanticargo (Sweden)	23,096	
Lykes (US)	21,160	
Gulf Europe/HL (International consortium)	49,559	
Sub-total	946,437	85.9
Non-conference lines		
Polish Ocean (Poland)	68,016	
Contract Marine (US)	21,600	
Amco (US)	22,100	
Falline (Canada)	9,600	
ABC (Belgium)	17,400	
Balt Canada (USSR)	5,256	(0.5)
Arctic Line (USSR)	11,700	(1.1)
Sub-total	155,672	14.1
Total	1,102,109	100.0

(2)   the outsider will restrict liftings to a certain volume, perhaps the status quo;

(3)   shippers will not forfeit loyalty rebates when using that particular outsider.

Tolerated outsider status is often an interim stage pending admission to the conference.

Soviet firms have had this status on several liner routes at various times and perhaps the major current example is the North Europe – Caribbean service. Baltcapas is run by the Baltic Shipping Company and is serving Central America, Jamaica and Venezuela from North Europe. It is a non-conference service having 'tolerated outsider' status with the Association of West India Transatlantic Steam Ship Lines.

Baltcapas employs conventional vessels of the Baltic Shipping Corporation in the 13,000–14,000 dwt range. Semi container ships of 244 TEU with reefer capacity are also used. The usual schedule includes Leningrad and four ports in the Hamburg–Antwerp range but the pattern of Caribbean calls is more complex. Kingston alone is served by every sailing and vessels then go on to either Corinto and Acajutla or Santo Tomas de Castilla, Port Limon and Cristobal. There are occasional calls at three other ports. The large number of disparate ports in the Caribbean makes meaningful analysis difficult. Few services, of the many going to the area as a whole, call at the same set of ports. For the same reason it is not possible to present satisfactory figures for shares of route capacity. Some typical transit times for the Soviet and other lines can, however, be compared (Table 5.19).

Baltcapas transit times are around or above the average. Reliability on this route is very variable; the range is from 0.43 to 19.00 days off schedule. Of the twenty-six conventional operators Baltcapas comes sixteenth with an average 7.15 days

Table 5.19
Transit Times on the North Europe–Caribbean Trade
(October 1982 to September 1983)

Kingston from Hamburg – ranked 2nd of 3 operators	
fastest	18.9 days
Baltcapas	23.9 days
slowest	26.7 days
Kingston from Rotterdam – ranked 1st of 3 operators	
Baltcapas	20.6 days
slowest	23.4 days
St Tomas from Hamburg – ranked 2nd of 4 operators	
fastest	26.5 days
Baltcapas	27.9 days
slowest	39.6 days

delay. All unitized services are more reliable than this, the worst being 6.20 days behind schedule. Baltcapas frequencies are also low except for Hamburg and Kingston.

The 32 members of the Association of West India Trans-atlantic Steamship Lines (WITASS) have been concerned about Soviet competition for some time but the Baltic Shipping Company service is long established. The conference is more concerned about other, speculative competitors whose names, ship types and destinations change at 'a bewildering pace' (WITASS Annual Report, 1982). Negotiations between WITASS and the Soviet company have led to agreement but the details have not been publicized. It appears that the link 'falls short of giving the outsiders "tolerated" status but shippers will not forfeit loyalty arrangements if the non-conference companies are used' (Lloyd's List, 16 December 1983). According to Lloyd's *Export Shipping*, (vol. 2, no. 3 (1984)), Baltcapas now has 'tolerated outsider status'. The agreement covers two areas:

(a) Westbound to the Islands section (smaller islands in East Caribbean) and north-east coast of South America.

(b) Scandinavia, Hamburg/Bordeaux range, and UK west-bound to Dominican Republic, Haiti, Jamaica, Nether-lands Antilles, east and west coasts of Central America and Panama.

The Baltcapas service clearly has put pressure on the conference which has accepted them to the extent of offering tolerated outsider status, or something approaching it. Without the details of the agreement it is difficult to assess how serious the Soviet competition is regarded. British operators are not involved except to the extent that they are also cross-traders carrying continental cargo.

5.8 Soviet liner service combining conference and outsider operation

5.8.1 Balt Levant, Scan Levant and Rinela lines

The Balt Levant and Scan Levant services from North Europe

to Eastern Mediterranean are operated by the Estonian Shipping Company of Tallinn. They are in effect one service and the Scan Levant name appears to be used simply to market the service in Scandinavia. Fortnightly sailings are offered using a pool of obsolete conventional tonnage built in the 1950s and 1960s and around 4,400 deadweight tonnes. Rinela Line, part of the Latvian Shipping Corporation, offers a fortnightly container service with a modern fleet including the Kapitan Tomson class of 333 TEU RoRo/container vessels and 490 TEU fully cellular ships of the Simon Bolivar class.

The following itineraries are normally adopted (occasional calls in brackets):

BALT LEVANT/SCAN LEVANT	RINELA
Tallinn	Riga
(Oskarshamn)	Aarhus
(Sarpsborg)	(Gothenburg)
(Moss)	Antwerp
Hamburg	Rotterdam
Rotterdam	London
Dunkirk	(Piraeus)
(Bilbao)	Limassol
(Leixoes)	Beirut
Piraeus	Lattakia
Limassol	Iskenderun
Beirut	
Lattakia	
Mersin	
Istanbul	

Soviet transit times on the route are generally fairly long though the Balt Levant service and Rinela services from Hamburg and London to Piraeus are among the fastest (Table 5.20).

Of the nine unitized operators to Greece Rinela was the least reliable. It was on average 6.83 days off schedule, the best operator being only 1.33 days behind. In contrast Balt Levant and Scan Levant are ranked first and second of the seven lines offering conventional services to Greece, although no line provided a particularly high standard of service. Balt Levant averaged 4.69 days behind schedule and Scan Levant was 7.43 days off.

Table 5.20
Transit Times on the North Europe–Eastern Mediterranean Trade
(February 1983 to January 1984)

Piraeus from Rotterdam – ranked 6th and 8th out of 8 operators		
fastest	Norasia	9.5 days
slowest	Rinela	21.4 days
Piraeus from London – ranked 1st and 5th out of 5 operators		
fastest	Rinela 2	10.1 days
slowest	Rinela 1	19.8 days
Piraeus from Hamburg – ranked 2nd of 5 operators		
fastest	Navibulgar	16.8 days
	Balt Levant	18.2 days
slowest	Prodromos	22.0 days

This is an example of the Soviet Union serving part of the route as a conference member and part as an outsider as they are members of the Levant conference but this covers only a section of the range that they serve. Rinela uses modern, well-equipped vessels and achieves some highly-competitive transit times. On the other hand it also has some excessively long transit times and is the least reliable container operator. Balt Levant/Scan Levant, despite using elderly vessels, achieve above average transit times and better reliability than their conventional competitors.

5.9   Trans-Siberian Container Service

While the Trans-Siberian Container Service (TSCS) is essentially land based it is important to include it in any analysis of Soviet shipping as it succesfully captures what would otherwise be seaborne liner cargo between Europe and the Far East. It provides the shortest surface route for Europe – Far East cargo and as early as the 1920s a transit cargo tariff from Europe to Japan was available. Modern container shipments began in 1967 though significant volumes were not carried until the early 1970s. The container service can be conveniently divided into three segments: seaborne movement from Far Eastern countries to Soviet Pacific ports, the Soviet railway system and the European end (Figure 5.1).

81

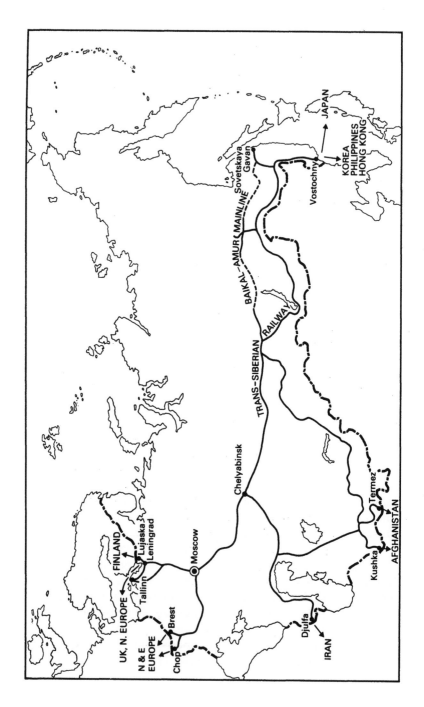

Figure 5.1 The Trans-Siberian Container Service.

When the service was in its infancy the Far Eastern end consisted of two old converted timber carriers of about 6,000 tonnes deadweight carrying mainly twenty-foot boxes from the Russian port of Nakhodka to Japan, calling at Kobe, Yokohama, Osaka and Nagoya with a maximum monthly capacity of 630 TEUs. At this time Nakhodka had one container berth with a single thirty-tonne portal crane. It was heavily congested with bilateral Soviet trade and must have been the weakest link of the service. Expansion has been on a vast and rapid scale. A new port, Vostochny, has been constructed and this now deals with most traffic. Its facilities include a container park of four million square feet, four rail-mounted Transtainers, twenty straddle carriers and three side loaders. A four track branch line leads to the Trans-Siberian Railway (TSR). Nakhodka has expanded and now has two Mitsubishi rail-mounted gantry cranes but massive growth is planned. The port of Vladivostok has also been used at times.

The shipping service is operated jointly by the Soviet Far East Shipping Corporation (FESCO) and the Japanese lines, Yamashita-Shinnihon and Iino. Eleven ships of between 138 and 824 TEUs provide frequent calls at ten ports, mainly Japanese. Kobe and Yokohama receive eight per month, Hong Kong, six. Direct calls are also made at Pusan in Korea. Considerable bottlenecks at the Soviet ports have been a major problem. Equipment breakdown, often due to severe weather conditions, is common and some consignments have reportedly taken 100 days to reach their destination.

The core of TSCS is the railways. The Trans-Siberian Railway (TSR) stretches from Moscow to Vladivostok via Chelyabinsk, Novosibirsk and Lake Baikal. The Far Eastern section passes close to the Chinese border then heads southwards to Vladivostok. The distance from Moscow to Nakhodka is 9,441 kilometres and the journey time for the 'fast' passenger train is ten days. TSCS block trains join the mainline via branches to the Pacific ports. Boxes consigned to Iran and Afghanistan leave TSR at Chelyabinsk and travel by rail to the borders where road transit takes over. For other destinations much of the traffic goes through Moscow. The block trains are composed of fifty or fifty-five flatbed wagons each capable of carrying two TEUs and are hauled for most of the journey by electric locomotives.

The European part of the journey is divided by transport made into three services – Transrail, Transea and Tracons.

Transrail service involves continued transport on Soviet railways to the USSR border where containers are transferred from the broad Soviet gauge to standard gauge European wagons. There are four crossing points of which the main ones are Chop (on the Czech border) and Brest (on the Polish border). Most traffic to West Germany, the largest customer, is carried this way.

Transea involves rail transit to a Soviet port then transfer to a container vessel for shipment to the final destination. The ports are: Zhdanov on the Sea of Azov for Italy, Spain and Yugoslavia; Leningrad for the Continent and UK; Tallinn for Norway, Denmark and Sweden; and Riga for France and Portugal. Also it is thought that a little Mediterranean traffic goes by train to Trieste or Ravenna, then by ship. The British ports of call are usually Hull, Tilbury and Ellesmere Port. Services from the Baltic ports are operated by the Soviet Baltic and Latvian Shipping Corporations with seven ships varying in size from 62 to 358 TEUs.

Tracons is a lorry service. Containers are transferred to Skoda, DAF and Leyland Trucks at Vysoko Iltovsk near Moscow and are delivered to consignees mainly in Germany, Austria, Northern France and Switzerland. It is claimed that this is the fastest service with a quay to house transit time of 28–35 days from Japan to West Germany.

TSCS operations are in the hands of v/o Soyuztransit (or SOTRA), a subsidiary of the Soviet Ministry of Transport. Commercial aspects of the system are controlled by individual firms, seventeen in all, who negotiate contracts with Soyuztransit. These organizations, usually Japanese forwarding agents, are granted licences by the Soviet Union and are known as Non-Vessel Operating Common Carriers (NVOCCs). They canvass for cargo and offer their own rates usually based on a seven class tariff. The dominant NVOCCs are Jeuro Container Transport, Pracht and Mollers. Jeuro, as senior NVOCC acts as a general agent co-ordinating bookings and passing them on the SOTRA. Soyuztransit charges the NVOCCs a flat rate per box to each major destination regardless of commodity. The flat rate tariffs have been estimated to be between 40 to 60 per cent of the inclusive rate charged by the NVOCCs to the shipper. One example, a forty-foot container from Japan to London, had an all-in rate of US $4,000 charged to the shipper which included US $2,370 charged by Soyuztransit (Sangian, 1984).

Each of the NVOCCs using the Trans-Siberian service is competing with the Far Eastern Freight Conference (FEFC) lines as well as the other outsiders on the Europe–Far East route. They have been able to undercut FEFC tariffs by up to 30 per cent on some commodities though their rates are argued to be higher than the conference in some cases. In fact comparison is very difficult as the NVOCCs' tariff is so much simpler than their conference competitors' pricing system. Whatever price advantage the service may have it suffers from a poor reputation for service quality, especially for reliability, transit times and security. Attempts to improve the service have been a partial success; a computer-based container tracing system has been installed, faster trains are being used and handling capacity in the ports has improved (LSE, 1985).

The TSCS has gained a substantial share of Far East trade but is much more successful in some areas than others. It suffers a major eastbound–westbound imbalance: the cargo flow from the Far East is three times that in the reverse direction. One reason for this is that since the outbreak of the Iran–Iraq war large volumes of Iranian imports from the Far East are carried on the railway. Between 1980 and 1984 Iranian imports on TSCS averaged 37,000 TEU annually, about a third of the total. There are no equivalent containerized exports from Iran so the reverse flow is of mainly empty containers.

The main Far Eastern source and destination of TSCS traffic is Japan. It has had little success in Korea, Hong Kong, Taiwan and the Philippines where non-conference seaborne competition is strong. But China is now relying increasingly on the TSR for its trade with Western Europe and Scandinavia, since it offers a fast alternative to sea transport (Lloyd's List, 26 October 1985). Transit times between Europe and China have averaged only 35 to 37 days. At the European end, the German Federal Republic is the largest recipient of cargo accounting for over 14 per cent of the total TSCS traffic, including Iran. The European Community as a whole takes around a third of TSCS westbound shipments. Finland, Norway and Sweden are also important and this reflects the fact that no FEFC lines call direct at these countries; the gain in terms of distance, and in some cases transit time, of using the railway is greatest here.

Since 1980 there has been no significant growth in total TSCS transit cargo though eastbound liftings from Europe have improved. Future expansion will depend on increased railway capacity within the Soviet Union. The Trans-Siberian Railway is very intensively used but the new Baikal–Amur Mainline (BAM) is offering it some relief for part of its length while at the same time generating new traffic (Figure 5.1). The Chinese are also building a new rail link from Urumchi to the TSR to be opened in 1987. Overall capacity could also be increased by improving efficiency and speed. Soyuztransit see theoretical current capacity as being 200,000 TEU per year in each direction and have argued that it could be raised to 600,000 TEU in fifteen years. Total cargo flow in both directions reached nearly 200,000 TEU in 1983 though the total has been lower in subsequent years. This decline results from the highly competitive posture adopted by shipping conference outsiders, such as Evergreen and Yang Ming who can offer similar rates but better service quality. Capacity figures are in fact of little value; the Soviet railway and port system is capable of handling very large volumes of container through-put and the amount available for transit cargo will be affected by, among other factors, the degree to which Soviet internal and bilateral shipments are given priority.

The Trans-Siberian Container Service is undoubtedly a major competitor in the North Europe–Far East liner market. In 1984 its liftings accounted for 5 per cent of eastbound and 6 per cent of westbound liner trade (Graham and Hughes, 1985). It has the combined advantages of short distance (compared with the seaborne trade), a simple rates structure and fairly low prices. Although other non-conference operators such as Evergreen can provide higher standards of service quality it is still a successful operator to Scandinavia and parts of Central Europe where seaborne operators have less of a transit time advantage.

5.10   The impact of Soviet shipping in the liner trades

There can be little doubt that when operating as outsiders Soviet lines undercut conference rates. This is normal for outsiders. They must compete with established conference members who have a marketing advantage and who offer rebates and other inducements to keep shippers' and agents' loyalty. Despite the paucity of published evidence there are many instances, some of which have been mentioned earlier, where Soviet lines undercut the discounted conference rates in certain markets by more than 20 per cent. In fact, Soviet lines behave no differently than other outsiders. Moreover in many trades it is other outsiders, often operating faster and more modern vessels, who are the price leaders rather than the Soviets. For instance, early in 1985 Morflot Freight Lines, general agents in Canada for the Arctic Line and Balt Canada, announced an increase of sailings to two a month between Montreal and certain European ports. Rates were to be about 10 per cent below conference levels which rose substantially when CAST, a Canadian owned outsider, was admitted to the conference in January 1985 (Lydolph, 1985). Prior to joining the conference it was CAST not the Soviet lines who had been the price leader in this market. In other markets too, Soviet rates are matched or even surpassed by other outsiders. Thus on Europe – Far Eastern trades rate-cutting has not been confined just to the Soviet Balt Orient line. Norasia (West German with chartered Greek tonnage) and Cosco (Chinese), as well as the Taiwanese companies Yang Ming and Evergreen, have been heavily rate-cutting. When Yang Ming began its Far East–Europe services early in 1983 it was accused of undercutting rates by up to 40 per cent in order to break into the market and capture market share (Lydolph, 1985). In this it succeeded and conference member carryings dropped substantially during 1983.

Where Soviet lines are members of the relevant conferences they often appear anxious to maintain conference rates at high levels. They are members of the Levant Conference (Levcon) which covers the route from the Hamburg/Antwerp range to Syria and the Lebanon. On this route the Soviet line argues that it has tried to push up the rates which, during 1984 and 1985, it considered too low. Soviet shipping company officials claim that it was they who suggested the introduction of currency adjustment factors and standard terminal handling charges within this conference.

Rates represent a key competitive factor but not the only one. Rates offered by any liner operator must be seen in conjunction with the service quality provided in terms of frequency, transit times, reliability and specialized facilities. The preceding analysis shows that Soviet lines score poorly in all these respects. Whether operating as conference members or outsiders their services are generally slow, relatively unreliable and in many cases operated by smaller and older vessels. On routes where Soviet lines belong to the relevant conferences (Section 5.5 above) their transit times are average to poor compared to those of their competitors. They are worst on the routes to West Africa and best on services to the east coast of South America especially from Hamburg. Where Soviet lines operate as outsiders (Section 5.6) their reliability appears relatively poor while their scheduled transit times are average or slow. On the Europe to South East Asia routes, where Soviet outsider services are considered to be a major threat, one finds that Soviet transit times are particularly slow. Balt Orient also has the worst reliability record despite using their most modern fully cellular vessels on these Asian routes. Moreover, these vessels are small by comparison to those of the conference members and of the larger outsiders such as Evergreen. In essence, shippers or agents taking advantage of lower non-conference rates offered by Soviet lines are paying for a poorer service. Put in a different way, rate-cutting by Soviet lines may be partly or even totally necessary in order to off-set the poorer quality of Soviet liner services when compared to those of their major conference competitors.

The final question that one needs to consider is the extent to which Soviet outsider operations are a cause of the chronic instability in many liner markets. However, there is a problem in attempting to identify the causes of any instability. Given that various factors are constantly changing on a given route, how can an affect be said to have been caused specifically by Soviet competition? Trade levels and therefore load factors vary because of macro-economic causes in the countries concerned. Other operators increase and decrease capacity. Conference freight rates vary frequently as currency and bunker adjustment factors (CAFs and BAFs) change and as a result of special cargo quotes (SCQs) for specific commodities or customers. Freight rates in general and special quotes in particular are confidential. There is also the problem of 'illegal' rebating by lines within a freight conference. This is frequently widespread and, coupled with misdeclaration of cargo to enable a low freight rate to be charged, gives another possible but hidden cause of instability on a route.

As well as there being a multiplicity of causes of instability on a conference route, actually defining what it is and how it manifests itself is difficult. At its most serious one could find the break-up of a conference or bankruptcy for several lines on the route. Conference break-ups are uncommon and largely restricted to trades involving the United States. US Anti-Trust laws stipulate that conferences must be 'open'. That is, they must allow freedom of entry into and of exit from the market, and file tariffs with the US Maritime Administration. This has tended to make trans-Atlantic and trans-Pacific conferences prone to rate wars and collapses. Otherwise collapses are few and Soviet lines have not been accused of causing any specific break-up of a conference.

In cases of shipping lines ceasing to trade or becoming insolvent this is not normally caused by problems on one route. Many liner shipping companies trade on various routes and are involved in other parts of the shipping industry and other industries. This has become widespread since containerization. Such diversification often prevents collapse. Again, there have been no accusations of lines being put out of business primarily through Soviet competition.

Only one case of a vessel being withdrawn from trade specifically because of Soviet competition has been identified, and here the Far East Shipping Company (FESCO) was only one of the causes. The Australian National Line (ANL) withdrew one of its six ships, the Australian Enterprise, from the trade to Hong Kong, Taiwan and the Philippines in 1983 blaming the 'predatory policies' of outsiders 'in particular the subsidised FESCO line of the USSR' (Seatrade, 1985). In fact trade volumes overall had been falling and ANL ship utilization was down to between 56 and 60 per cent of capacity. Coupled with this the conference share of the trade was falling as a result of competition from three main outsiders of which FESCO was only one. The Israeli national line Zim Israel Navigation and the Panamanian-registered, Chinese crewed Hong Kong Islands Line (HKIL) were, along with the Soviets, undercutting conference tariffs by 10 to 15 per cent or even up to 40 per cent on certain commodities. ANL's problem was, however, short-lived. Three months after the withdrawal of their ship and following pressure put on the three outsiders by governments and unions agreement was reached with the conference. Zim and FESCO accepted quotas on both the northbound and southbound trades and agreed to undercut by no more than 5 per cent. The Soviet line agreed to greater reductions in cargo levels than Zim and HKIL simply agreed to remove one of four ships from the trade for a minimum of six months. FESCO had been operating on this route for many years, always as an outsider. It appears that only in combination with two other outsiders and during a period when the market was particularly depressed was there a serious problem for an established conference line.

In conclusion it is clear from the earlier analysis that in most liner markets Soviet outsiders provide a relatively small share of the total capacity available. On the Europe to North American Eastern Seaboard routes, Balt Canada and Arctic Line provide less than 2 per cent of the capacity while Balt Orient offers only about 4 per cent of TEU capacity on the Europe – Far East trades, though the Trans-Siberian railway link provides a further 12 per cent or so. Of the routes analysed, only on Europe – East Africa does a Soviet outsider provide a major share of the capacity and that is only 15 per cent. On Europe – Far East trades Evergreen and Yang Ming, both relatively new outsiders, provide three times as much TEU capacity as Balt Orient, while on North Europe to Eastern

Seaboard CAST, another relative newcomer who has more recently been admitted to the conference, operates four times as much tonnage as the two small Soviet outsiders. In so far as overcapacity is one of the major causes of liner market instability, it would be difficult to attribute such overtonnaging largely to Soviet participation when Soviet lines generally offer a relatively small share of the total capacity.

CHAPTER SIX

Carrying the Soviet Union's Own Direct Trade

6.1 Bilateral shipping agreements

The strength of the shipping links between the Soviet Union and its many trading partners varies. This chapter examines these links, first by reviewing shipping agreements between the Soviet Union and other countries; secondly, by concentrating on UK–Soviet trade.

The Soviet Union has the opportunity to control shipment for all of its exports and imports. All international sales and purchases are directed through the agencies of the Ministry of Foreign Trade. By buying foreign goods on 'free-on-board' (FOB) terms but selling Soviet exports on 'cost, insurance and freight' (CIF) terms they could ensure that the method of shipment is always in Soviet hands. In many cases this is done but the Soviet government appears to have been aware of the concern expressed on this issue by foreign shipowners and governments. In order to maintain a dialogue on shipping matters Joint Shipping Commissions have been set up with many major non-communist trading partners. Representatives of government and the relevant shipping industries are members of the commissions and regular meetings are held. Commissions exist between the Soviet Union and, for example, Netherlands, Norway and Greece in Europe and India, Brazil, Zaire, even the Cape Verde Islands in the developing world. The commissions provide a forum for countries to press for better deals in direct trade. In some cases this has led to joint shipping services of various types as the following examples illustrate.

France This trade is covered by a governmental agreement dating from 1967. The Service Maritime Combiné Franco-Sovietique was established between the Latvian Shipping Company and Compagnie Générale Maritime (CGM). This links Le Havre/Dunkirk and Riga with fortnightly sailings and Dunkirk and Ventspils every three weeks. Two CGM ships are employed in addition to vessels from a pool of Latvian Ro-Ros. A second joint service exists between the French Compagnie Meridionale de Navigation and the Black Sea Shipping Company serving Marseilles and Odessa.

French shipowners are unhappy with the system as only 8 per cent of seaborne volume is carried in French vessels. Despite frequent talks with the Soviet Union no progress towards evening out the trade has been made. The 1967 agreement provides for fair shares in volume and value of cargo to the ports covered by the joint service. French owners argue that the Soviet lines get around this in three ways. First, they route 60 per cent of French liner traffic via foreign ports, especially Antwerp and Rotterdam, or other French ports not covered by the agreement. Secondly, they insist that much of the capital equipment and plant exported by France is carried on Soviet river/sea ships so that it can be taken directly to its inland destinations. Thirdly, the tariff for containers is so low as effectively to exclude French operators (Lloyd's List, 27 September 1985). According to French shipowners, French ships in 1984 carried only 1 per cent of the total 7.6 million tonnes of imports by sea from the Soviet Union and 19 per cent of the 5.3 million tonnes of exports. It is because their overall share is only around 8 per cent that early in 1986 the French government gave notice of its intention to withdraw from the agreement unless this imbalance was corrected.

Germany As part of the bilateral shipping agreement with West Germany there is a Soviet German Joint Baltic Liner Service with three members: Bruno Bischoff Reederei of Bremen, Horn-Linie of Hamburg and the Lithuanian Shipping

Company. This conventional and container service has two itineraries connecting both Bremen and Hamburg with Klaipeda. The Bremen service provides two to three sailings weekly using three Soviet and two German conventional vessels which carry a few containers. Hamburg is served every two weeks with one German vessel. The combined services therefore provide a substantial annual capacity of 16,000 TEU plus conventional space. Despite the joint service it has been estimated that three-quarters of this trade is carried on Soviet vessels (Department of Trade, 1979).

Belgium A joint service between Belgium and the Soviet Union is offered by the Latvian Shipping Corporation in association with Ahlers Lines of Antwerp. Only one vessel is provided for the service and this is a small conventional liner owned by the Soviet partner.

Japan One of the earliest joint shipping services was established in 1958 by the Far Eastern Shipping Company of Vladivostok and the Japan Nakhodka Line. The latter is a consortium of three major Japanese lines: Yamashita-Shinnihon, Kawasaki Line and Iino Line. The Soviet and Japanese lines have equal cargo shares in this part of USSR–Japan trade which has grown from 45,100 tonnes in 1958 to 302,800 tonnes in 1982 (*Soviet Shipping*, 1983). Both lines each contribute two vessels to the service. The FESCO vessels are both of 7,400 dwt and the Japanese have one of 7,400 dwt and a smaller 4,600 dwt vessel. But this joint service covers only a fraction of the 3 billion roubles of trade between the countries. One estimate of cargo sharing allocates 97 per cent of traffic to Soviet vessels (Department of Trade, 1979).

India There is a bilateral trading agreement between the Soviet Union and India, its biggest trading partner in the developing world. Links followed Indian independence starting with supplies of steelworks equipment from the Soviet Union. The value of the trade is still increasing, for example from one billion roubles in 1979 to 2.5 billion in 1982. Liner cargo is very important: Soviet exports include machinery, paper and fertilizers while their imports are dominated by

94

jute, tea, coffee, hides, fabric and shoes. Bulk shipping is growing, particularly exports of oil and oil products to India and imports of rice and wheat (*Soviet Shipping*, 1984).

Agreement to establish a joint line was reached in 1966 and the service now has four participating firms: the Black Sea Shipping Company on the Soviet side with the Shipping Corporation of India, the India Steamship Company and the Scindia Company. The system ensures equality of liftings and earnings for the lines. Furthermore, since 1976 it has been extended to all commercial cargoes rather than just liner traffic. The link with the bilateral trade agreement also means that there is no room for cross-traders on the route.

6.2   UK – USSR trade links

The UK is one of the main non-communist trading partners of the Soviet Union. There is over a billion US dollars worth of trade in each direction in most years and in foreign exchange terms it has been fairly well balanced. In tonnage terms, however, there is a large imbalance; in some years British imports are up to ten times the volume of British exports (Table 6.1). Inbound trade is dominated by bulk cargoes, particularly those carried by tanker. British exports are, in contrast, predominantly liner oriented. As a result the liner trade is itself imbalanced. In the period 1982 to 1984 Soviet liner exports to UK have been only a little over half the figure for the corresponding flow in the opposite direction.

Soviet vessels dominate the trade between the two countries. In recent years they have never carried *less* than 65 per cent of Soviet imports and 73 per cent of their exports to the UK. British lines have never carried *more* than 17 per cent of UK exports and 12 per cent of UK imports. Usually the UK figures are rather less and apply to all cargo types. Surprisingly in all the trades, cross-trading vessels carry a much higher share of both imports and exports than British vessels do.

This small British share contrasts notably with the performance of UK lines in other direct trades. Despite the decline of the UK fleet in recent years, British liners continue to carry between a quarter and a third of UK imports and exports in all

Table 6.1
Recent UK–USSR Trade (000s tonnes)

Year	UK imports	UK exports
1977	6,256	232
1978	6,336	523
1979	4,081	400
1980	2,294	380
1981	2,202	583
1982	3,721	324
1983	3,957	430
1984	4,252	827

Source: Business Statistics Office (1985).

of the near and short-sea trades. But more significantly on such routes the cross-trader share would normally be large. The Soviet link has a very small cross-trader share and what there is appears generally in the form of a cross-Channel or North Sea ferry flying the flag of an EEC country with the cargo continuing its journey overland through Europe.

The UK share of the relatively large volume of tanker cargo shipped from the Soviet Union is very small too. In some years no UK vessels have been involved and it was not until 1984 that their participation reached a meagre 4 per cent (Table 6.2). The volume of tanker exports from the UK is insignificant. Dry cargo imports from the USSR have been increasing in volume terms recently after a substantial fall in the late 1970s but the share carried on British vessels remains very small. The UK share has not recovered, however, and does not exceed 5 per cent.

Table 6.2
UK Imports from the USSR by Nationality of Vessel, 1984

Cargo type	Volume (000s tonnes)	% carried by nationality of vessel		
		UK	Soviet	Others
Dry bulk	720	4	76	20
Liner	180	9	70	21
Tanker	3,352	4	78	18
Total	4,252	5	77	18

Source: Business Statistics Office (1985).

Table 6.3
UK Exports to the USSR by Nationality of Vessel, 1984

Cargo type	Volume (000s tonnes)	% carried by nationality of vessel		
		UK	Soviet	Others
Dry bulk	434	2	70	18
Liner	375	8	89	3
Tanker	18	11	79	10
Total	827	5	78	17

Source: Business Statistics Office (1985).

Because of its high value the liner cargo part of Anglo-Soviet trade is of particular importance. British lines have carried only around 8 per cent of exports and 9 per cent of imports of this category in recent years (Tables 6.2 and 6.3). Cross-traders have achieved somewhat higher liftings while the remaining 60 to 90 per cent of liner traffic in tonnage terms is carried by Soviet lines. Much of the liner cargo between the two countries is carried by a joint Anglo-Soviet shipping service. The Baltic Shipping Company (BSC) of Leningrad, one of the largest Soviet shipping corporations, operates the service with the United Baltic Company (UBC), a subsidiary of the British company Andrew Weir & Co. The Latvian Shipping Company (LSC) of Riga had operated a separate service to the UK but it joined the Joint Service in January 1985. The service is on three routes and uses three vessels (Table 6.4).

Although there is a twenty-five year history of co-operation between UBC and Morflot a pooling system was not estab-

Table 6.4
The Anglo-Soviet Joint Service, 1985

Route	Line	Vessel	Type	Capacity (TEU)
Tilbury–Leningrad	UBC	*Baltic Osprey*	FC[1]	155
Hull–Leningrad	BSC	*Mekhanik Evgrafov*	RO[2]	154
Ellesmere Port– (Dublin)–Riga	LSC	*Inzhener Kreylis*	RO	247

[1] Fully cellular container ship.
[2] Roll on–roll off ship.

lished until 1982 following pressure from Britain for equal shares in the trade. The full cost, revenue and tonnage pool is thought to be unique among Soviet shipping agreements outside the CMEA countries. It ensures parity of revenues even though UBC provides only a third of the capacity. The service applies a value-related commodity tariff of 250 items using box rates. Increases in the tariff are cost related and are reviewed annually.

Together UBC indicates that the three lines carry 72 per cent of liner type cargo though these figures differ from UK official statistics. FOB and CIF cargo is allocated to the pool partners but because the pool involves revenue sharing, and fixed rates the Soviet line is indifferent as to which pool members actually carry the freight. The remaining 28–30 per cent of liner cargo, apart from the small amount of European transit cargo, is carried on ad hoc sailings of Soviet vessels to Hull and Tilbury. Typically these are one way voyages involving loads such as 400 cars being imported to the UK. As it is a one way trade UBC is not anxious to take on responsibility for it. The joint service is not involved with the Trans-Siberian Container Service transit cargo. Typical eastbound cargoes include chemicals, glass and machinery. New cars are one of the major westbound items.

In conclusion, it is evident that despite the apparent enthusiasm for 40–40–20 cargo sharing the Soviet Union has been very successful in excluding foreign flag vessels from its trades. In a few cases the result of negotiations at Joint Maritime Commissions is a 50–50 split of trade, thus excluding any cross-traders. An important example is with regard to Soviet–Indian trade. In most cases, however, the Soviet Union appears to have manipulated the trade to the extent that almost all cargo is carried on Soviet vessels and this occurs even where there is a joint service as with UK, France and Japan. Soviet shipping officials have argued that most Soviet ports are open to vessels from all trading partners. It is argued by the president of the Murmansk Shipping Company that there are no laws or regulations restricting the participation of foreign-flag ships in the transportation of Soviet foreign trade cargoes, or introducing any discrimination in respect of any flag. He supports this argument with the fact that the port of

Murmansk was visited by 262 foreign vessels under the flags of nineteen nations during 1980 alone (*Soviet Shipping*, 1981). Despite the absence of any legal barriers it is clear that, where possible, the Soviet Ministry of Foreign Trade allocates Soviet cargo to Soviet vessels unless agreement on cargo sharing has been reached with the trade partner. By buying FOB and selling CIF the Soviets can always control means of shipment. It may also be the case that non-Soviet shipowners are reluctant to enter and compete in some of the bilateral trades because the rates are too low.

CHAPTER SEVEN

The Bulk Trades

7.1 USSR grain requirements and production

Soviet participation in the carriage of general cargo in the Soviet Union's non-bulk direct trades is disproportionately large (see Chapter 6). To what extent is this true of the bulk trades? To resolve this question the two major bulk trades affecting the Soviet Union, namely grain and oil shipments have been analysed in some detail.

Bulk grain is one of the largest commodity flows in world shipping. It accounted for 1,080 billion tonne-miles of shipping in 1983 compared with 1,400 for iron ore and 960 for coal (Fearnley and Egers, 1984). The term grain includes wheat; coarse grains such as maize (corn), barley, oats and rye; and, in addition, leguminous types such as sorghum and soya beans. Grain shipments have grown in importance in recent years. In 1970 they accounted for 4 per cent of world tonne-mileage, by 1980 this had risen to 6 per cent. Now 8 per cent of all commodities shipped fall into the grain category. Much of the increase has been caused by Soviet imports which have in turn been created largely by failure to meet Soviet targets for domestic production.

Grain requirements in the Soviet Union fall into several categories:

(1)   human grain consumption;
(2)   livestock feed;
(3)   seed;

(4)   industrial use;
(5)   dockage waste;
(6)   reserves;
(7)   export.

Demand for human consumption can be assumed to be fairly stable and has been estimated at 46 million tonnes per annum by the International Food Policy Research Institute (Desai, 1982). Grain requirements for seed and industrial use have been estimated at 30 and 4 million tonnes respectively. It is difficult to estimate dockage waste as this varies according to source, moisture levels and other factors affecting quality. The discount for dockage waste is likely to lie between 5 and 15 per cent of total grain supplied.

Grain requirements for livestock feed are very variable. Before 1971 Soviet policy was to slaughter prematurely meat and dairy cattle in years of bad harvest because of the predicted shortage of feed grains. This obviously inefficient policy has subsequently been replaced by one of importing grain on a large scale. Desai estimated animal feed requirements at 125 million tonnes for 1981/2, rising to 144 million tonnes for 1985/6.

Grain reserves are low as a result of numerous bad harvests but a small volume of purchases is committed annually to building up reserves. On top of this the Soviet Union has continued to export small volumes of grain to a number of satellite states, most notably to Cuba (Table 7.1). Although

Table 7.1
Soviet Grain Exports 1982 to 1984 (000s roubles)

	1982	1983	1984
Vietnam	5,807	—	5,966
North Korea	34,584	20,058	—
Cuba	155,052	138,761	155,498
Mongolia	4,213	4,390	—
Poland	65,358	68,442	83,529
Others	19,800	10,180	3,268
Total	284,814	241,831	248,261

Sources: Vneshnyaya Torgovlya SSSR, 1983 and 1984 (Ministerstvo Vneshneii Torgovli).

tonnage figures for export are not available it is thought that around two million tonnes per annum is committed to these satellite states. Around five million tonnes is put into reserves. Total demand for grain for all uses in the Soviet Union, including wastage, is therefore between 220 and 250 million tonnes per annum though as a long-run objective the Soviets appear to be aiming for one tonne per head of population. This would give a total of around 270 million tonnes.

In recent years Soviet grain production has fallen consistently below demand. The last substantial harvest was in 1978–9 when 237 million tonnes was supplemented by 15 million tonnes of imported grain. Since that year production has been well below target (Table 7.2). The shortage of

Table 7.2
Soviet Grain Production and Imports 1978–84
(million tonnes)

Grain year (July–June)	Soviet harvest	Imports	Total
1978–9	237	15	252
1979–80		30	
1980–1		34	
1981–2	175	46	221
1982–3	170	32	202
1983–4	195	33	228
1984–5	170	57	227

Sources: US Department of Agriculture; International Wheat Council.

home-produced grain has generally been caused by bad weather. For the grain year 1984–5 the problem has been one of drought. In the previous year the shortage was caused by heavy autumn rain in North and East Kazakhstan and Western Siberia. The rain delayed the harvest, leaving several million hectares uncut in mid-October and thus at risk of frost and snow (Lloyd's List, 11 October 1984).

7.2 Soviet grain imports

Since the policy of large-scale slaughtering of cattle after bad harvests has ended, the shortfall is now met by importing substantial quantities of grain. In the past the bulk of Soviet imports has come from the United States. A major five-year agreement was signed in 1975 under which a minimum of six and a maximum of eight million tonnes would be bought annually. The total would comprise equal amounts of wheat and maize. This was extended twice, each time for one year, and expired in 1982. In fact, much more than eight million tonnes was bought after further consultation and during the late 1970s the US supplied 50 to 75 per cent of annual Soviet import requirements. A new agreement was signed in 1983, again for five years. The Soviet Union will buy a minimum of nine million tonnes per annum and can buy up to twelve million without further negotiation. The total will be made up of wheat, corn and possibly soya (Lloyd's List, 3 September 1983).

The Soviet Union has also had an agreement with Argentina. Since 1980 it has taken 4.5 million tonnes per annum of feedgrains (mainly sorghum and maize) and soya under this five-year pact. Again, in reality much more has been imported, particularly wheat. An agreement announced in 1981 added a further twenty-five million tonnes of Canadian grain to potential supplies of imported grains. There was no annual commitment but the total will be supplied between 1981 and 1986. Australia has been seeking a similar commitment, but because of its large balance of payments surplus with the Soviet Union the latter favours a reciprocal agreement involving Soviet machinery.

In addition to its longer-term agreements, the Soviet Union continues to purchase grain in large single transactions. For example, a contract was signed in late 1983 for delivery of 1.5 million tonnes of wheat worth £155 million during the first half of 1984 (Lloyd's List, 22 November 1983). As well as grain supplied under long-term or large-scale agreement substantial volumes are bought in single lots on the international market. In some cases this has been done secretly, numerous purchases being made at advantageous prices. In 1972 twenty million tonnes of US grain was acquired in this way.

The volumes purchased from the different grain supplying countries vary from year to year and depend to a large extent on the credit and financial facilities offered to the Soviets. Even price variations of over 20 per cent between different sources of supply appear less important than the right financial packages. It is thought that the large volumes of Argentine grain supplied during the early 1980s partly resulted from deals with European banks.

Grain imports by source are summarized on Table 7.3. Over the last five grain years the Soviet Union has imported an annual average of 40.2 tonnes, making it by far the largest buyer in the world. Its nearest rivals are Japan (25.1m tons), China (13.4) and Mexico (6.4). It is a particularly important market for Argentina, taking up to 80 per cent of that country's grain exports. What must also be stressed is that grain purchasers in such countries as Japan are numerous but the Soviet contracting is done by one agency of the Ministry of Foreign Trade.

Table 7.3
USSR Grain Imports by Source (million tonnes)

Supplier	1978/9	1979/80	1980/1	1981/2	1982/3	1983/4	1984/5
Argentina	1.4	5.1	11.1	13.4	9.6	6.9	8.1
Australia	0.1	4.0	2.9	2.9	1.0	1.5	3.2
Canada	2.1	3.4	6.8	9.2	8.9	6.3	8.4
EEC	0.2	0.9	1.2	2.2	—	4.4	8.8
US	11.2	15.2	8.0	15.5	6.2	10.4	22.3
Others	0.1	1.8	4.0	2.4	6.3	3.3	5.8
Total	15.1	30.4	34.0	45.6	32.0	32.8	56.6

Sources: *Lloyd's Shipping Economist;* US Department of Agriculture; International Wheat Council.

7.3   Shipping Soviet grain imports

Given that there are enormous volumes of grain moving long distances to the Soviet Union, there are important shipping implications. The Soviet bulk carrier and OBO fleet is relatively small. It comprises 161 vessels aggregating 2.9 million gross tonnes (1985) which accounts for only around a tenth of the Soviet fleet and only about 2 per cent of the world tonnage of ore and bulk carriers in 1985 (Table 3.6 above). Furthermore, this small fleet of bulk carriers is dominated by vessels in lower size categories: 78 of the 161 vessels are under 15,000 tonnes and 124 are below 20,000 tonnes. The average size of Soviet bulk carriers at about 15,000 grt is only half of the UK average (Table 3.5 above). Apart from grain, the deep-sea movement of dry bulks is not a significant requirement of Soviet trading activity. Their exports of major dry bulk commodities tend to be with neighbouring countries and are either shipped overland or by short-sea means. It should be added, however, that as well as grain becoming a regular deep-sea import commodity, coal is now shipped deep-sea over such distances as Soviet Far East to North Europe, though in much smaller quantities.

The Soviet Union has reacted in several ways to the need to transport substantial quantities of grain over long distances despite the shortage of Soviet bulk carrier capacity. Much of its own bulk fleet spends most of the year carrying grain and some attempt is being made to increase tonnage with new-buildings and second-hand purchases. But since fleet expansion is slow, some grain is bought with the proviso that the exporter arranges carriage of a proportion of the total volume purchased. Most important of all has been an enormous expansion of chartering, including time, voyage and bareboat charters.

Estimates have been made of how much grain the Soviet fleet *can* carry during a period. However, a more useful measure is what they actually do carry as their priorities for vessel deployment include other routes and cargoes. To estimate Soviet grain carryings during 1983 Lloyd's Shipping Information Services data were analysed. The port-to-port movements of all Soviet bulkers over 3,000 gross tonnes listed by Lloyd's were examined and movements from grain exporting areas to the Soviet Union were identified. Vessels making brief calls at non-Soviet ports en route, after sailing from a grain exporter, were included. These were assumed to be for bunkering or taking on supplies. The results of this analysis were aggregated and compared with Soviet grain import totals for 1983 (Table 7.4).

This shows that during 1983 the Soviet Merchant Marine handled no more than about 10 per cent of bulk imports direct

Table 7.4
Estimate of Soviet Grain Imports Carried
in Soviet Vessels during 1983 Calendar Year

Exporter	Total Soviet grain imports (000s tonnes)	Sailings of Soviet bulk carriers. Aggregate net tonnage	Estimated grain capacity* (tonnes)	% of total imports carried in Soviet vessels
Australia	991	105,000	210,000	21.2
Argentina	8,000	115,000	230,000	2.9
Canada	9,049	701,000	1,402,000	15.5
USA	7,636	270,000	540,000	7.1
Total	25,676	1,191,000	2,382,000	9.3

* Based on an average of 50 cublic feet per tonne of grain given that much of the Soviet import figure is of wheat and other heavy grains. Note that wheat requires around 48 cubic feet per tonne and maize occupies 50 cubic feet per tonne.

from exporting countries to the USSR. In addition some grain is transhipped at Rotterdam and Soviet vessels sailing from a grain exporter to the Netherlands would not have been included in the analysis. Few cases of this have been identified though in 1982 1.4 million tonnes of Russian grain passed through the port. The likely explanation is that chartered vessels were used to carry grain as far as Rotterdam, where it was transhipped to enable Soviet tonnage to be used for the final leg. It should also be noted that the Soviet Union bought a number of second-hand bulk carriers during 1983. This would have added to their grain-carrying capability and the lag between buying the vessel and the change of name and flag being entered on the Lloyd's computer may have meant that a small amount of grain could have been missed out.

Even allowing for this it would appear that around 90 per cent of Soviet grain importing requirements have to be met with vessels chartered in. In 1980 it was estimated that Soviet vessels could meet only 7 per cent of their requirements and the cost of chartering deep-sea tonnage was estimated at US $500m (LSE, 1984).

The Soviet bulk carrier fleet has been expanded substantially over the last three years. In 1983 when the market for second-hand bulkers was depressed sixteen vessels totalling over a half a million deadweight tonnes were bought. These vessels were in the range 26,000 to 45,000 dwt and, with the exception of three, were under seven years old. Fifteen of the sixteen were picked up from North-West European or Hong Kong-based owners. The total cost was estimated at $130m (LSE, 1984). During the same period three newbuildings were added to the bulk fleet. Second-hand purchases were also made during 1984, including some ex-UK twelve-year old vessels of handy size. In the year to mid-1985, nine bulkers averaging 25,000 tonnes gross were added to the fleet.

Soviet activity in the charter market is always shrouded in secrecy. Though it would be fair to add that it is generally difficult to get reliable information on chartering, sources at the Baltic Exchange in London have said that the Soviets are almost obsessed with confidentiality. It is thought that any broker passing on information about Soviet clients is unlikely ever to work for them again. Soviet interest lies in two sectors of the market, handy-sized bulk carriers between 20,000 and 46,000 tonnes and Panamax-sized vessels up to about 70,000 tonnes. Their approach to the market ranges from voyage charters of single vessels to time charters of groups of vessels for periods up to a year. The following quotes from the Baltic Exchange Correspondent at Lloyd's List serve to illustrate this:

> The Soviet business, although impossible to confirm as always, was rumoured to involve a 60,000 tonner taken from Gibraltar for a transatlantic round voyage at $4,700 daily, and a 64,000 tonner from the Continent to the Baltic at $4,500. (Lloyd's List, 2 October 1984).

> Following weeks of speculation, sources said the Soviet Union had hired around two dozen Greek flag vessels in the last month to carry grain from the US Gulf to the Soviet Union. It was believed that most of the fixtures had been arranged in Piraeus with the vessels varying from handy up to Panama size. Moreover, said sources, an estimated 15 vessels had been taken for periods up to July 1985 at rates ranging from $3,150 daily to between $4,200 and $4,300 daily. (Lloyd's List, 21 July 1984)

The real extent of Soviet chartering remains unknown, though a US forecast stated that, taking a 50,000 tonne dwt bulker as the average in trans-ocean grain trade, there would be 500–800 voyages to Soviet grain-handling ports each year during the 1980s.

As well as normal voyage and time charters, some bulk tonnage is acquired on an unusual bareboat charter/hire purchase arrangement. Because the only purchaser (with very few exceptions) of foreign goods in the Soviet Union is the Ministry of Foreign Trade, the Ministry of Merchant Marine cannot buy ships itself. The process of finding a second-hand vessel suitable for purchase, informing the Ministry of Foreign Trade and going through the bureaucratic mechanisms to arrange the buying of the ship often takes too long. By the time the Ministry is ready to buy the vessel it may already have been sold or the requirement may no longer exist. As a result, the Ministry of Merchant Marine through Sovfracht, its chartering arm, has devised a scheme whereby the vessel can be effectively bought over a long period and with Western finance during which it is on a bareboat charter. The periods are thought to be typically three to five years.

7.4   Impact of Soviet grain imports on freight rates

The importance of Soviet participation on the international grain market and therefore on the tramp market cannot be overestimated. It is by the far the largest single buyer of grain and the largest single charterer of tramp ships.

Its influence on grain prices is probably limited because most grain produced worldwide is grown to meet a known level of domestic demand and is not traded internationally. The agricultural policies of grain producing countries are more likely to influence levels of supply than the possibility of sales to the Soviet Union. Prices of grain differ between countries even where the commodity is exported (Table 7.5). Soviet consumption does, however, reduce what would otherwise be a very large world surplus of grain. Even with Soviet demand grain stocks have stood at around 200 million tonnes during the 1980s.

Table 7.5
Average Export Prices of Wheat and Corn in US Dollars
per Tonne Free on Board for Calendar Years 1980–2

	1980	1981	1982
Wheat			
Argentina	203	189	188
Canada	209	211	192
US Gulf	175	177	171
Australia	176	175	162
Corn			
Argentina	147	137	114
US Gulf	130	134	117

Source: US Department of Agriculture.

On the other hand, Soviet grain trading has undoubtedly influenced the dry cargo market. Tramp shipping is close to the theoretical model of perfect competition in many of its features, notably it has no very large sellers among the thousands of shipowners involved. On the buying side, however, Soviet activity has been held responsible for rises in the rates prevalent for vessels in certain sectors of the market. For example, large volumes of grain were shipped from Argentina to the Soviet Union in the spring of 1982 resulting in a spate of large-scale chartering, mostly in the handy-sized range, which caused a temporary recovery in rates in this sector of the market. A recovery was also detected throughout

Table 7.6
Impact of Heavy Soviet Chartering on
Typical Single Voyage Rates, 1982 (US$ per tonne)

	Soviet chartering activity		
	Before Jan/Feb	During Mar/Apr	After May/Jun
Grain: 30,000 dwt from			
US Gulf to Japan	18	24	19
Coal: 55,000 dwt			
Hampton Roads to Japan	17	19	16
Iron Ore: 120,000 dwt			
Brazil to Continent	6	7	5

Source: Lloyd's Shipping Economist, vol. 4, no. 7 (1982).

the market, although in a more diluted form with larger vessels (Table 7.6). Brokers estimated that at least one million dwt was picked up during the March and April period (*Lloyd's Shipping Economist*, 1982). The impact on rates at and around the ports from which Soviet grain is shipped is likely to be greater.

It is not possible to identify the causal impact of Soviet demand on increased freight rates over longer periods. Record imports occurred in the grain year 1981/2 when the total reached 46 million tonnes compared with 35 in the previous year. On the charter market generally, however, 1981 was characterized by tumbling rates. The dollars per tonne figure for grain from US to Japan for handy-sized bulkers fell from thirty-eight to twenty. The period contained so many other factors, not least a substantial increase in supply as new-buildings became available, that increased Soviet demand appeared to have no impact over the full year. But without it, it is likely that freight rates would have fallen even further. Soviet chartering has continued to benefit operators in the dry cargo market. The Dry Cargo Review of 1985 was headed 'USSR interest saves the market from "catastrophe"' (Lloyd's List, 2 January 1986). A few months earlier the same news-paper had suggested that '. . . significant gains on the (Baltic Freight) Index have coincided with reports of fresh Soviet fixing. For instance the near 25-point leap logged on Oct. 20 followed reports that the Soviet charterers had accounted for perhaps as many as 80 vessels of varying sizes in the preceding weeks.' (Lloyd's List, 30 October 1984)

It should be added that as well as being particularly secretive, Soviet charterers try to spread their business widely throughout the market. This is presumably done to lessen the impact of their involvement in terms of freight rate rises. They will not want to cause an increase in rates while still engaged in further chartering.

In summary, Soviet demand for grain creates substantial derived demand in the dry cargo market. This is strongest in two sectors: handy-sized and Panamax bulk carriers. Freight rate increases can be detected during periods of large-scale chartering for long-distance movement. Chartering to ship grain from Argentina to the USSR would have a greater impact than shipping to the same volume from US to USSR because the supply of shipping tonnage would be reduced for a longer period. It is not possible to identify Soviet influence on freight rates over long periods but undoubtedly if they were not active on the market, freight rates would be even lower than they have been during the last few depressed years. Dry cargo operators have benefited from reduced volatility in the market due to regular Soviet chartering.

Finally, one sad reflection on the state of Soviet grain trading: after years of bad harvests and imports on an unprecedented scale, the agency responsible for purchasing grain abroad is still called Eksportkhleb or Export-Bread!

7.5 Soviet participation in the oil trade

The Soviet Union is the largest oil producer in the world, accounting for 20 per cent of global output. The increase in Soviet production has been phenomenal. In 1955 only 70 million tonnes was produced compared with 616 in 1983. Over three-quarters of Soviet production comes from Western Siberia and the Volga–Ural area. The latter has now passed its peak production and the bulk of output for the next few years is likely to come from the Tyumen area of Western Siberia.

Demand for oil and oil products within the Soviet Union is considerable and has grown rapidly though energy conservation measures and the increased use of natural gas as a substitute have steadied the situation. Internally, oil is transported by road, rail and sea but the most important means is a complex network of pipelines.

Soviet exports of crude oil and petroleum products make a notable contribution to its balance of payments. In 1984 they were valued at nearly 31 million roubles. There is also a small Soviet oil import trade for certain types of crude oil but the volume of this trade has declined since the oil price rises of the mid-1970s and is now of little significance.

Pipelines are used for oil exports as well as for internal shipping and these cross the border into Eastern Europe at two points. Eastern Europe accounts for over 40 per cent of Soviet oil exports, most of which are moving by pipeline.

Table 7.7
Soviet Oil Exports by Destination, 1984 (million roubles)

Area		Oil and oil products exported (million roubles)
Eastern Europe		13,533
Western Europe		13,356
Others		
Afghanistan	120	
Vietnam	380	
India	1,067	
North Korea	104	
Cuba	1,325	
Morocco	92	
Mongolia	158	
Ethiopia	139	
Japan	138	
Miscellaneous	484	
Sub-total		4,007
Total		30,896

Source: *Vneshnyaya Torgovlya SSSR za 1984g.*

Western Europe consumes almost as much Soviet oil as do the countries of Eastern Europe (Table 7.7). Only two non-European consumers of any significance exist: India and Cuba each bought over one million roubles worth in 1984. Exports to OECD countries have grown during recent periods despite the general decline in oil trade worldwide. A 15 per cent increase was registered betwen 1982 and 1983 as OECD consumption of Soviet oil reached 1.57 million barrels per day.

Soviet oil is marketed through Sojuznefteexport whose subsidiaries Euronefta, Internefta, Vostoknefta and Dalnefta sell to Western Europe, the CMEA members, Africa and US/Japan respectively (*Lloyd's Shipping Economist*, 1983). These firms apparently operate on a normal commercial basis to the extent that prices are charged in line with those prevalent internationally and discounts are offered to regular customers. Japanese oil trading companies also buy and sell Soviet oil. Large volumes of Soviet exports are of refined products rather than crude. In 1983 around 43 per cent of OECD imports were in products form.

Despite the importance of oil exports to the Soviet Union its tanker fleet is unimpressive in size and quality. There are very few large vessels in the fleet. But as much of the oil export trade is in products form few would be needed. The largest are seven tankers of 150,000 dwt and no others exceed 50,000 dwt. There are few modern tankers in the fleet. Many are so old that they are unable to be chartered out becuse they do not meet the latest safety standards. Over half of the fleet is more than fifteen years old compared with only 16 per cent of the world fleet. As a whole the tanker fleet is small, accounting for only 19 per cent of Soviet tonnage compared with 34 per cent worldwide. Only 11 of the world's 400 bulk/oil carriers fly the Soviet flag.

The need for a large fleet is in fact lessened by the close proximity of many of the country's buyers of oil. Only India and Cuba are a deep-sea voyage away. Attempts have been made to lessen capacity on the Cuban trade through 'oil swap' agreements. The Soviet Union has encouraged Venezuelan and Mexican producers to supply Cuba direct in exchange for Soviet oil being shipped to European customers. In 1978 Petroleos de Venezuela agreed to swap 10,000 barrels per day with the Soviets supplying a West German refinery part-owned by the Venezuelan company. This arrangement work-ed successfully for several years.

Such moves have helped the Soviet fleet to meet a large part of the country's oil transport requirements. An analysis of exports to various European countries shows that between a third and 85 per cent of oil from the Soviet Union was carried in Soviet vessels in 1983 (Table 7.8). Soviet participation is relatively low in the largest single export trade which is to Italy and also low on the Finnish trade. In contrast Soviet vessels dominate on the German and buoyant Dutch trades.

Some Soviet shipping companies even charter out tonnage. The OBO (ore/bulk/oil) ships of the Novorossiysk company are frequently advertised as being available for charter. However, Soviet chartering in has become a common feature of the tanker market over the last two years. Requirements to haul gas oil and other petroleum products from Black Sea and Baltic ports have occurred at the rate of up to six per week on the exchange in London. Many appear to be for vessels in the

Table 7.8
Soviet Oil Exports by Flag of Vessel for 1982 and 1983

Importing country	1982		1983	
	Capacity provided (million dwt)	% Soviet flag	Capacity provided (million dwt)	% Soviet flag
Netherlands	17.2	89	15.8	84
Scandinavia	3.9	84	4.6	77
West Germany	1.4	100	2.9	84
Italy (from Black Sea)	18.4	49	20.3	43
France	9.6	66	11.9	77
Finland	8.5	—	9.8	37
Greece	5.0	—	7.6	65

Source: *Lloyd's Shipping Economist*, vol. 6, no. 3 (1984).

20,000 to 40,000 dwt range. Although this has been stepped up recently some Soviet chartering in and out has continued from the early 1970s.

The Soviet merchant marine is able to meet a large part of oil transport requirements with its rather dilapidated tanker fleet. Increasingly, however, vessels are being chartered in as exports increase. This trend is likely to continue as Morflot tankers become obsolete and are scrapped. There are few tankers on the Soviet order-books. This move may well be deliberate. The tanker market remains in deep recession with considerable surplus capacity. Sovfracht can take advantage of low tanker freight rates while Soviet shipyards are kept busy building vessels for which there is higher priority.

CHAPTER EIGHT

The Soviets and the Cruise Markets

8.1 Cruise ship controversy

Soviet cruise vessels have been operating through UK ports for over twenty years. It is only since about 1980, however, that such operations have aroused the same kind of criticism among British shipowners as Soviet liner services have done over a much longer period. The present chapter sets out to examine the scope and nature of Soviet cruise ship operations, particularly in the UK cruise market, and the impact of such competition in the various markets.

The views of UK operators on the issue have been summarized by the General Council for British Shipping as follows (GCBS, 1984):

1 UK operators do not object to foreign competition in their home market, providing ships operate according to normal Western commercial standards.
2 Their concern is the volume and heavily subsidized nature of Soviet competition.
3 In recent years, the Soviets have injected unilaterally into a static market substantial increases in the number of cruises and berths offered at prices which no Western operator working to normal economic standards can hope to match. The end result can only be a trading down across the entire market place.

4   Commercial companies cannot fight the resources of the Soviet state on their own. Only strong Government action can be effective. That is why the General Council of British Shipping on behalf of UK operators has urged Government action unless the Soviets limit their involvement to a far greater extent than so far.

5   The alternative would be the eventual demise of the UK home-based cruise fleet with the attendant loss of ships, several thousand jobs, repair contracts, balance of payment contributions and back-up for national defence needs.

The main critics of Soviet cruise operations in Britain are Cunard and P & O. Cunard is interested primarily in the upper end of the market and concentrates many of its sailings from the United States where there is no Soviet participation. P & O is more clearly in direct competition with Soviet cruise lines as it offers many mid-price cruises for British holiday-makers. But a substantial volume of P & O's capacity is for the upper end of the market on board such vessels as the new *Royal Princess*. Since CTC, which markets Soviet cruises in the UK, is clearly aiming for the lower end of the market, competition with P & O is also likely to be limited.

There has been intense lobbying of Parliament and government by British cruise lines. Operators claimed early in 1983 that Soviet fares could be as little as 40 per cent of the minimum British equivalent and facilities were as good as the British counterparts. They stated that only poor marketing prevented the Soviet lines from gaining a larger share. It was claimed that Soviet operations aimed to earn foreign exchange and undermine Western shipping (Lloyd's List, 28 January 1983). The then British Minister for Shipping responded by claiming that agreement had been reached limiting berths offered on Soviet cruises in 1983 to no more than 2 per cent over the 1982 figure. The British lines were not satisfied with this and wanted a decrease in berths offered by the Soviet lines. British goverment policy, however, continued to concentrate on encouraging commercial negotiations rather than intervening directly. Talks were held but no solution was reached.

CTC lines pointed out the advantages for Britain of Soviet cruise calls. Around £2 million is spent annually on harbour dues, bunkering and provisioning at British ports, mainly Tilbury (Lloyd's List, 16 February 1983). In addition valuable refit work has been undertaken by British Shipbuilders. As criticism of CTC's operations was mounting during early 1983 the prospect of £20 million of refit work was held out by the Soviet passenger ship organization, Morpasflot. Such contracts are regarded as very valuable by British Shipbuilders. In 1982 Tyne Shiprepairers refitted the cruise vessel now called *Leonid Brezhnev*. The contract reportedly provided 600 jobs for six months. The counter-argument from the British lines was that the threat to British seafarers' jobs was also great. They added that refit work placed by domestic owners greatly exceeded the value of the Soviet work (Lloyd's List, 19 February 1983). Perhaps one should note here the extent to which both P & O and Cunard have used yards on the continent and in Scandinavia for cruise shipbuilding, repairing and refitting rather than British yards.

Despite the apparent lack of success of the commercial negotiations CTC offered, in late 1983, to reduce supply of berths by 25 per cent. Although the British liners were not appeased the government seemed quite pleased by this (*Daily Telegraph*, 4 January 1984). The cutback led a Conservative backbencher to question the shipping minister on what he saw as a move likely to deprive people on low incomes of the opportunity to go cruising (Lloyd's List, 5 and 6 December 1983).

A further offer this time to cut capacity by nearly 7 per cent was made by CTC in early 1984. The British lines demanded a greater reduction. Since then a change of course for British policy has begun to emerge. As part of the 1984 Shipping Bill there are plans to extend the powers of retaliation against unfair competition. Retaliatory measures have been available since the 1984 Merchant Shipping Act was passed but these were for cargo shipping and were never used. A draft document included plans for such powers to be extended to cruise shipping and this is clearly aiming at CTC though the line is not mentioned by name (Lloyd's List, 25 June 1984).

Some governments have taken a stronger view than the

British. Soviet cruise ship operations were banned from the United States and Australia as a result of the invasion of Afghanistan. The Australian ban has now been lifted and two vessels were deployed there during 1985 carrying an estimated 15,000 passengers. In April 1983 the Italian and Soviet governments reached agreement to reduce Soviet operations, which amounted to over 40 per cent of the Italian market. This stemmed from Italian foreign exchange curbs and concern over the large number of unemployed seamen. Under the agreement Italian tour operators will not be allowed to charter vessels for more than 250 days per year and it was planned to reduce the figure to 200 days in 1984 (Lloyd's List, 29 April 1983).

8.2   Soviet participation in the cruise market

Cruise holidays on Soviet ships are offered in Britain by CTC lines. Formerly called the Charter Travel Club, this firm was absorbed by the Anglo-Soviet Shipping Corporation in 1974 (Seatrade, 1976). Vessels are time chartered from Soviet shipping corporations by CTC who advertise the sailings mostly from Tilbury to Tilbury though ports such as Dover and Swansea are occasionally incorporated into the schedules. The extent of Soviet participation in the British market can be seen in Tables 8.1 and 8.2.

Interest in carrying foreign cruise passengers dates from the

Table 8.1
Vessels Chartered to CTC Lines during 1984 and 1985
for European Operation

Vessel	Berths	Line	Period (months) 1984	1985
Mikhail Lermontov	550–600	Baltic Shipping Co.	10.0	1.5
Taras Shevchenko	600–650	Unknown	—	9.0
Leonid Brezhnev	500	Black Sea Shipping Co.	10.0	10.0
Mikhail Kalinin	200	Baltic Shipping Co.	8.0	—
Armenia	200	Unknown	1.5	—

Sources: 1984 and 1985 CTC Lines brochure.

Table 8.2
Capacity Offered by CTC out of UK Ports

Year	Bednights
1977	119,125
1978	93,175
1979	97,160
1980	161,140
1981	178,080
1982	206,938
1983	250,480
1984	179,280
1985	165,520

Sources: Lloyd's List, 9 December 1983, and later issues.

early 1960s when a French travel agent began bookings. Since then a large number of organizations have become charterers, tour operators or ticket agents for Soviet cruises. One of the largest is Neckermann Reisen (NUR) of Frankfurt. In 1963/4 they provided 2,500 cruise holidays on Soviet vessels; by 1978/9 they carried 20,000 passengers. NUR is only one of several German firms using Soviet vessels. A list of firms and

Table 8.3
Major Western Tour/Travel Agencies Selling Soviet Cruises

Independent western firms

Yamashita	Japan
DDSG	Austria
NUR Touristic	W. Germany
Touropa	W. Germany
Seetour	W. Germany
Transtour	France
Grandi Viaggi	Italy
Italturist	Italy
Bumerang	Turkey
FZD	Finland

Western firms wholly or partially Soviet-owned

CTC Lines	UK
Transocean	W. Germany
Dolphin	Italy
Uniorient	Japan

Source: Soviet Shipping, vol. 4, no. 3 (1984).

countries involved in Soviet cruising is shown in Table 8.3.

In the United Kingdom the Russians are competing for a share of a small and specialized market consisting of about 50,000 passengers a year (Table 8.4). In addition to the 50,000 passengers taking cruise holidays from the UK about 25,000 take fly–cruises. Of this 25,000, roughly half fly to the Mediterranean and half to the Caribbean. The Russians compete in both the direct and fly–cruise sectors. In 1984 they offered three Mediterranean fly–cruises plus seven Oriental ones. They also offer a small number of one-way voyages with a flight in the opposite direction.

Table 8.4
British Residents Taking Cruise Holidays from UK, 1984

Line	Passenger per annum (approx)
CTC	9,000
Cunard	9,000
Fred Olsen	4,000
P & O	25,000
Others	3,000
Total	50,000

Although, as Table 8.2 indicates, a substantial amount of Soviet capacity sails from UK ports, many cruise itineraries include calls at continental ports to pick up European passengers. Soviet vessels carry about 60 per cent of West German cruise holiday-makers. Of the seven cruises aboard the *Mikhail Lermontov* during 1984, three, including the round-the-world cruise, also called at Rotterdam. Other vessels call at Rotterdam, Amsterdam or Zeebrugge on many sailings. Tour operators presumably keep a quota of berths for European passengers on such voyages which must reduce capacity available for the British market.

Much of the controversy around Soviet cruise operations rests on how many cruise passengers are actually being carried by CTC and how many of those would otherwise use a UK cruise line. The approximate figures in Table 8.4, provided by a source close to the industry, suggest that about 18 per cent of the direct (i.e. non-fly cruise) UK market is taken up by

CTC. Their share of the fly–cruise market would be rather smaller. By comparison P & O have about 50 per cent of the UK market.

But the British lines also argue that massive amounts of capacity are being dumped by CTC. In fact it appears from our own surveys in 1985 that a substantial part of the capacity of vessels calling at UK ports is not available to UK passengers. On a summer 1985 cruise to the Canary Islands the *Mikhail Lermontov* carried 94 continental passengers, accounting for 16 per cent of its capacity. In addition 450 British citizens were carried giving the 600 berth ship a load factor of 91 per cent. The same vessel's next itinerary was a Baltic Capitals fly–cruise. Of the 407 passengers embarking at Tilbury, around 150 were US and Canadian citizens who had flown to London to join the ship. Additional European passengers would have been taken on at Rotterdam.

Another vessel competing in the UK market is the *Taras Shevchenko* with a capacity of around 650 berths. This is one of two vessels which together met the bulk of CTC's requirements for the 1985 season. It undertook fifteen cruises advertised for the UK market ranging from a round-the-world tour down to six night mini-cruises and most included a call at a continental port such as Rotterdam or Amsterdam to embark and disembark continental passengers. Figures for UK calls have been obtained and, as Table 8.5 shows, reveal that only about half of total capacity is taken up by British passengers. A note of caution should be expressed when discussing capacity figures. The simple nature of the accommodation on Soviet vessels, with large numbers of upper bunk beds, are not necessarily suitable for their predominantly elderly clientele (Saga Holidays for the over 60s are major users). Furthermore the large numbers of four, five and six berth cabins on Soviet vessels prove unpopular on the Western market. This means that a vessel sailing at less than capacity may effectively be described as full. Allowing for this it is still significant that passengers boarding in the UK only occupied around half of the Soviet vessel's capacity in 1985.

The cruise shipping market is highly concentrated with around 50 significant operators having an estimated 200 vessels. There is strong market segmentation both geographi-

Table 8.5
British Holidaymakers on CTC Cruises Aboard
Taras Shevchenko, 1985

Brochure reference number	Cruise	Duration (nights)	UK passengers Adults	Children	% of total capacity occupied by UK passengers (assuming 650 berths)
1	Data unavailable				
2	Caribbean	28	130	3	20
3	Mediterranean fly–cruise	11	203	6	32
4	Data unavailable				
5	Mediterranean fly–cruise	11	197	9	32
6	Brittany	6	164	14	27
7	Madeira	14	221	11	36
8	Northern Capitals	13	468	—	72
9	Tenerife	13	547	—	84
10	Data unavailable				
11	Brittany	6	508	—	78
12	Northern Capitals	13	427	—	66
13	Tenerife	14	410	20	66
14	Oslo/Copenhagen	7	315	—	48
15	Mediterranean fly–cruise	12	205	—	32
	Average		316	5	49

cally and in terms of price. The two main areas for cruise shipping are the Caribbean, aiming mainly at the US market where competition is intense, and the Mediterranean/North Atlantic. Others are Norway, the US West Coast–Alaska, South-East Asia and round-the-world cruises. Many operators specialize in only one or two of these areas.

There is also a tendency to specialize in one price sector of the market. The top end is characterized by Scandinavian owners of luxurious tonnage such as Royal Viking Line of Norway with the vessels *Royal Vikings Sea, Sky* and *Star*. Their 1984 tariff ranged from £1,075 to £49,619 (the lowest price is for the eight-day Southampton to New York sailing). At the lower end are Greek owners of older tonnage, such as Chandris. Their tariff for the *Romanza* ranged from £205 to £749 for summer 1984. Even within the same cruise vessel there is a considerable difference in price from, at the top end, 'penthouse' or 'deluxe' suites down to inside four-berth cabins without shower/toilet. The former can be five to seven times the price of the latter. Soviet cruise shipping operators on the international market fit in at the lower end though they are not always the cheapest. They are probably the only operators still attempting to market five and six berth cabins.

8.3   A comparison of Soviet and other cruise fleets

The Soviet fleet of passenger vessels suitable for cruising is the largest in the world. While Japanese tonnage of ferries and passenger vessels exceeds the USSR figure, it is predominantly a ferry fleet (Table 8.6). Five of the Soviet shipping companies run passenger ships: the Black Sea, Baltic, Far Eastern, Murmansk and Northern (Soviet Shipping, 1985). The fleet is however co-ordinated by the general passenger agency, Morpasflot. The passenger fleet comprises between seventy and eighty vessels providing 23,000 to 25,000 berths. This makes Morpasflot as a whole the world's largest cruise ship operator though each Soviet shipping company's cruise

Table 8.6
Ferry and Passenger Vessel Fleets of Over 500,000 GRT, 1985

Flag	Gross tonnage	% world tonnage
Japan	1,074,326	13
USSR	643,004	8
UK	635,343	8
Norway	591,888	7
Greece	570,997	7
Italy	537,116	6
Sub-total	4,052,674	49
Rest of the world	4,278,301	51
Total	8,330,975	100

Source: Lloyd's Register of Shipping, *Statistical Tables* (1985).

123

Table 8.7
Largest Cruise Ships Operators – Number of Berths, 1983

Costa Armatori	Italy	7,298
Cunard	UK	4,470
Holland America	US	4,151
Norwegian Caribbean	US	4,808
P & O	UK	4,243
Royal Caribbean	US	3,844
Basic Soviet Fleet		13.659
Soviet fleet appearing in Lloyd's Voyage Records		10,329

Source: Lloyd's List, Special Report: The Cruise Business, 7 April 1983.

fleet on its own would not be as large as the major Western operators (Table 8.7).

In tonnage terms, around 65 per cent of capacity is permanently or periodically operating solely for Soviet passengers and much of the traffic is short distance. But a step above the ferry services are short mini-cruises enjoyed by a large number of Soviet citizens. Routes such as Leningrad–Tallinn, Odessa–Yalta and Murmansk–Kola Peninsula are popular. Soviet cruise holidays are also popular and usually organized by tourism councils, trade unions or bodies such as the Bureau for International Youth Tourism Sputnik. Domestic prices are comparatively low, typically in the range 15–35 roubles per berth per day. Many Soviet workers are provided with *putyovkas* by trade unions. These are accommodation vouchers offering discounts typically from 30 to 50 per cent on holidays including cruises. In manufacturing industry and agricultural bonuses in the form of free cruises are sometimes offered.

The Russian cruise ship fleet has been built up from a number of sources. Traditionally vessels have been acquired second-hand from the West. Greenway's *Soviet Merchant Ships* (1980) lists nine passenger vessels built before 1940 and several of these are still thought to be in domestic use. These include the *Sovietskiy Soyuz* built in Germany in 1923 and under the German flag until 1950. The *Rossiya* was built in Germany in 1938 and has flown the German and British flags. The *Admiral Nakhimov* built in 1925 as the German vessel *Berlin*, sank in 1945 and was salved to become a popular choice

Table 8.8
Some Soviet Second-hand Cruise Ship Purchases

Vessel	Built	Previous name	Flag	Sold to USSR
Maksim Gorkiy	Hamburg, 1968	*Hamburg*	German	1974
Fedor Shalyapin	UK, 1962	*Franconia*	UK	1973
Leonid Sobinov	UK, 1962	*Carmania*	UK	1973
Odessa	UK, 1974	*Copenhagen*	Danish	1975

among Soviet holidaymakers until it again sank in 1986. Of the more modern vessels the largest came second-hand from the West; some examples are given in Table 8.8.

The *Belorussiya* class represents the most modern Soviet tonnage in the cruise ship category (Seatrade, July 1983). The five vessels were built in Finland and delivered from 1975 onwards. They are unusual in providing berths for over 500 passengers while also having substantial capacity for 256 cars and lorries via stern doors. It is thought that they were built as Black Sea passenger vessels. In some cases the car decks have now been converted into extra passenger space. This shows apparent bad planning in that more vessels of this type were built than were required. One of the vessels, the *Leonid Brezhnev*, is a mainstay of the cruising operation from Tilbury to the Caribbean, the Canaries, Norway and the Mediterranean. This ship had its car decks converted into cabins and public rooms at the South Shields based Tyne Shiprepair Company in 1982 for £4 million. A similar conversion of the *Kazakhstan* took place in 1984 and the *Azerbaidzhan* and *Belorussiya* are planned to undergo the same treatment in 1986 at the West German Lloyd Werft shipyard (Lloyd's List, 30 November 1985). As well as new and second-hand vessels from Western Europe the Soviet cruise fleet has two classes of East German built vessels.

The *Ivan Franko* class of five 700–750 berth ships was delivered from 1964 to 1972. Some of these vessels have been used for non-Soviet holiday-makers on cruises in the Mediterranean, Black Sea, Canaries and Norway. Around-the-world and Pacific Island cruise itineraries have also been followed by them. Several have undergone major refits to upgrade the accommodation and public rooms on board and as a result capacity has been reduced to around 550 berths. One such vessel was the *Mikhail Lermontov* which has been used extensively in the West Eurpean and Australian markets until it sank off New Zealand on 16 February 1986 while on a cruise out of Sydney.

The *Mikhail Kalinin* class of 18 passenger ships with 330 berths was delivered from 1958 to 1964. Only eight of these vessels appear on Lloyd's Voyage Records; the others, if still in existence, are assumed to operate within the Soviet Union. A nineteenth was transferred to the Soviet in 1976. Of the eight involved in international cruising the following schedules were typical of those followed in 1984:

Mikhail Kalinin	– Canaries, North Africa, Baltic, Mediterranean cruises from Tilbury and Zeebrugge
Armenia	– Cruises from Britain to Mediterranean and Baltic
Turkmenia	– South-East Asia and Far East operations from Singapore and Hong Kong
Feliks Djerzinskiy	– Far East.

Soviet cruise ships tend to be smaller than average. Their largest take 750 passengers but this figure includes six berth cabins. Worldwide there are 15 vessels with a capacity of over 1,000, none of them Soviet operated. These include:

Norway (ex S/S *France*)	1,896 berths
Queen Elizabeth II	1,815 berths
Canberra	1,706 berths
Scandinavia	1,600 berths.

Partly as a reflection of their smaller size, Soviet vessels lack the degree of luxury and sophistication found on many of the Western vessels. There tend to be fewer swimming pools and most are outdoor. Also there are fewer dance floors, shops and sports facilities than on the larger and most luxurious vessels. For their size even the larger Soviet vessels tend to be rather more basic than other vessels in the 500 to 700 berth category. The trend internationally towards highly luxurious passenger ships has included some 'five star plus' vessels of this size which are far superior to any Soviet ships.

8.4 Comparative analysis of cruise holiday prices

8.4.1 Cheapest prices per berth per night

The highly segmented nature of the cruise market and the wide variation in the nature and quality of the cruise product makes meaningful comparisons between cruise operators rather difficult. To try and overcome the problems of comparability two separate analyses have been conducted. First, the prices per day for the cheapest berths on a range of vessels have been compared. Notwithstanding the possibility that some of these might be loss leaders, such an analysis should provide a good indication of competitive advantage at the lower end of the market. The second analysis involves a

Table 8.9
Price per Cheapest Berth per Night for Selected
Cruise Vessels in 1984

Line	Vessel	Range of lowest prices from various cruises (£)	Average (£)
Upper band			
Norwegian Caribbean	*Sunward II*	100–107	104
Royal Caribbean	*Nordic Prince*	94–98	96[a]
Cunard	*Vistafjord*	50–120	92
	QE II	64–88	79
	Cunard Countess	67–73	69[b]
Mid-band			
Fred Olsen	*Black Watch*	45–56	50
P & O	*Canberra*	44–53	48
Lower band			
Chandris	*The Victoria*	44	44
	Romanza	29	29
Vacation Liners	*Vacationer*	33–36	35
Soviet Lines	*Leonid Brezhnev*	38	38
	Mikhail Lermontov	37–38	37
	Armenia	33	33
	Mikhail Kalinin	23–32	30

[a] Based on an exchange rate of £1 = $1.48.
[b] Includes return flight London–Caribbean/US.

127

comparison of the prices offered on different vessels for broadly similar cruises, that is cruises in the same geographical area and offering similar ports of call. The number of comparable cruises is fairly limited, so there is a limit to the number of price comparisons which could be carried out.

The range of lowest prices per berth per night for a typical selection of cruises offered aboard each vessel is shown in Table 8.9. The berth in most cases is one of four in an inside cabin with toilet and shower. Where possible, the flight part of a fly/cruise has been excluded.

Soviet cruise prices for the cheapest berths are very much lower than those of most UK and European cruise operators. They are less than half those on the more luxurious vessels. Clearly Soviet cruises fit in at the lower end of the market. Only Chandris Line and Vacation Liners offer similarly low prices though Fred Olsen and the P & O *Canberra* offer the middle range of prices. Further analysis of the major rivals in terms of price shows the extent to which they are comparable with Soviet cruises.

Vacation Liners offers holidays to British residents on the *Vacationer*, a small vessel converted from a container ship and providing very limited facilities. There are only 74 cabins, mainly two-berth, but an advantage for this small ship is that all cabins are large with outside windows. The ship maintains a fixed schedule on a weekly basis with the following itinerary:

> Gibraltar;
> Portimao, Portugal;
> Seville, Spain;
> Tangier, Morocco;
> Malaga, Spain;
> Gibraltar.

Many passengers combine a week aboard with a week in Gibraltar. The vessel is registered in the Netherlands and sails with Dutch officers. The line has been operating very successfully since 1982 and has ordered a series of similar, small vessels, purpose-built in Dutch yards (Lloyd's List, 9 February 1984).

Chandris Cruises operates two elderly vessels. *The Victoria* cruises the Caribbean all the year round, is 48 years old and provides 500 berths. The *Romanza* operates in the Mediterranean during the summer, is 45 years old and has 700 berths. Both have been modernized and offer standard facilities. Price comparisons are difficult to make as British holidaymakers are offered all-inclusive fly–cruises but there are exceptions. The £29 per night quoted in Table 8.9 for the *Romanza* is for a spring cruise around Italy from Rome to Venice calling at various ports including Malta and Dubrovnik. The price quoted is for a four-berth inside cabin with washbasin.

Clearly, in this sector of the market, there are lines operating with similar fare levels to those of the Soviet corporations. *Vacationer* is an unusual case; the vessel is modern and offers comfortable accommodation but entertainment facilities are much more limited than usual. Its owners operate it successfully, and under a regulated flag. Chandris Cruises use older vessels than the Soviet lines but offer similar levels of comfort, food and entertainment. They have operated successfully for many years but using either Greek or open registry flags. A partial explanation of the low prices charged by Vacation Liners and Chandris may be low costs achieved through fixed regular schedules.

8.4.2 Prices on comparable cruises

Comparisons between Soviet and other operators of similar cruises (in terms of route and number of days) have been made for the following areas and are shown in Tables 8.10 to 8.18.

(a) Around-the-world
(b) North Europe–Northern capitals
(c) UK–Mediterranean–UK
(d) Black Sea fly–cruises
(e) UK–Northern Norway–UK
(f) Mediterranean fly-cruises
(g) East Mediterranean fly–cruises
(h) London–Canary Islands–London

Table 8.10
Around-the-World Cruise 1984-5

Line	Royal Viking	CTC
Vessel:	*Royal Viking Sky*	*Mikhail Lermontov*
Departure point:	Fly London–Miami	Sail Tilbury
Number of calls:	Calling at 30 ports in 25 countries ending at Southampton	Calling at 24 ports in 21 countries ending at Tilbury
Length (days):	99	97
Departure date:	18.1.85	5.1.84
Full price range:	£13,305–49,619	£3,600–11,745
Typical price range:*	£14,761–21,889	£6,095–8,070
Typical mid-price:	£18,330	£7,083

* In this and subsequent tables 'typical' prices are for a berth in an outside double cabin with bath/shower and toilet.

Table 8.11
Northern Capitals Cruise 1984

Line	Cunard	CTC
Vessel:	*Vistafjord*	*Leonid Brezhnev*
Departure point:	Fly London–Hamburg	Tilbury–Rotterdam
Number of calls:	7	7
Length (days):	15	13
Departure date:	5 August	4 June
Full price range:	£1,750–6,430	£495–1,310
Typical price range:	£1,750–3,550	£605–945
Typical mid-price:	£2,650	£775

Table 8.12
UK–Mediterranean Cruise 1984

Line	Cunard	CTC
Vessel:	*QE II*	*Mikhail Lermontov*
Departure point:	Southampton	Tilbury
Number of calls:	8	8
Length (days):	12	14
Departure date:	7 October	12 August
Full price range:	£1,350–3,610	£530–1,720
Typical price range:	£1,525–2,175	£890–1,180
Typical mid-price:	£1,850	£1,035

Table 8.13
Black Sea Fly–Cruise 1984

Line	Cunard	CTC
Vessel:	*Vistafjord*	*Leonid Brezhnev*
Fly:	London–Genoa	London–Genoa
Number of calls:	9	7
Fly:	Genoa–London	Genoa–London
Dates:	29 April	8 September
Days:	14	14
Price range:	£1,385–4,990	£630–1,510
Typical price range:	£1,385–2,770	£970–1,115
Typical mid-price:	£2,078	£1,043

Table 8.14
Northern Norway Cruise 1984

Line	Royal Viking	CTC	Norwegian Caribbean
Vessel:	*Royal Viking Sky*	*Leonid Brezhnev*	SS *Norway*
Departure:	Southampton	Tilbury	Amsterdam
Number of calls:	9	8	7
Fly:	Copenhagen–London	arr. Tilbury	arr. Amsterdam
Dates:	15 June	17 June	26 July
Days:	12	15	14
Price range:	£1,561–5,450	£570–1,515	£1,315–6,845
Typical price range:	£1,716–2,479	£935–1,090	£1,905–2,345
Typical mid-price:	£2,020	£1,013	£2,125

Table 8.15
Mediterranean Fly–Cruise 1984

Line	Chandris	CTC
Vessel:	*Romanza*	*Leonid Brezhnev*
Departure point:	Venice	Genoa
Number of calls:	6	7
Length (days):	8	11
Departure date:	April–October	6 October
Full price range:	£393–749	£520–1,210
Typical price range:	£539–714	£785–900
Typical mid-price:	£626	£842

Table 8.16
East Mediterranean Fly–Cruise 1985

Line	Costa	CTC
Vessel:	*Eugenio C*	*Leonid Brezhnev*
Departure point:	Genoa	Genoa
Number of calls:	6	7
Length (days):	10	11
Departure date:	2.10.85	19.10.85
Full price range:	£578–1,193	£560–1,305
Typical price range:	£957–1,143	£850–970
Typical mid-price:	£1,073	£945

Table 8.17
Canary Islands Cruises 1984

Line	Fred Olsen	CTC	P & O
Vessel:	*Black Watch*	*Mikhail Lermontov*	*Canberra*
Departure point:	London	London	Southampton
Number of calls:	6	6	6
Length (days):	13	14	13
Departure date:	22 December	22 December	23 December
Full price range:	£670–1,760	£520–1,695	£650–1,937
Typical price range:	£930–1,350	£880–1,165	£1,092–1,573
Typical mid-price:	£1,140	£1,023	£1,333

Table 8.18
Canary Islands 1985

Line	Fred Olsen/Cotsworld	CTC
Vessel:	*Black Prince*	*Taras Shevchenko*
Departure point:	Dover	Dover
Number of calls:	5	8
Length (days):	14	14
Departure date:	28 November	3 September
Full price range:	£299–965	£460–1,450
Typical price range:	£559–799	£745–1,005
Typical mid-price:	£655	£895

There are currently no Soviet vessels operating solely within the Caribbean and it has not been possible to identify comparable South-East Asian cruises. For each of the eight comparable cruises key features are listed in the accompanying tables. These include the typical price for a berth in an outside twin-berth cabin with toilet and bath or shower. Details are taken from 1984 and 1985 brochures.

A note of caution on the price comparisons must be made. Discounting by cruise lines is common. Group discounts are normal and both standby schemes and special offers are also found. Travel operators often charter ships for single voyages or make block bookings at advantageous rates. For example, Saga Holidays frequently use Soviet vessels and prices are lower than CTC themselves charge for the same cruise. CTC offer discounts of up to 10 per cent if fares are paid in full well in advance. Prices in some cases are fully inclusive. In others the journey to and from the ship may be extra. On CTC ships even coffee after meals is an additional expense.

For the selected routes the typical mid-range price for an outside double cabin on the Soviet vessel as a percentage of its competitors is shown in Table 8.19. For the more expensive and up-market cruises, 'typical' Soviet prices are generally around 50 per cent or less than those of their competitors. For cheaper cruises, Soviet prices are much closer to their competitors' and at times even higher. Examination of CTC and competitors' prices in individual routeings and in the summary (Table 8.19) shows CTC has two distinct market postures.

When competing with those cruise lines reputed to be operating at the top end of the market, such as Cunard, Royal Viking or the Norwegian Caribbean Line, CTC prices are way below those of their competitors (Tables 8.10 to 8.14). The typical CTC mid-range prices for a berth in a double outside cabin with bath/shower and toilet are generally only a third to a half those of their up-market competitors. But closer examination of the price ranges suggests that the real price differentials are very much wider. On a number of comparable cruises, the highest CTC price is lower than the lowest price of its competitor. Thus the highest price one could pay on the *Mikhail Lermontov* for a round-the-world cruise was

133

Table 8.19
Soviet and Western Pricing on Similar Cruises, 1984 and 1985

Competing operator	Cruise	Approximate duration	Soviet price as a % of competitor's
Royal Viking Line	Around-the-World	3 months	39
	Northern Norway	2 weeks	50
Norwegian Caribbean Line	Northern Norway	2 weeks	48
Cunard	Mediterranean	2 weeks	56
	Black Sea fly–cruise	2 weeks	50
	Northern Capitals	2 weeks	29
Fred Olsen	Canary Islands	2 weeks	90
P & O	Canary Islands	2 weeks	78
Fred Olsen/ Cotsworld	Canary Islands	2 weeks	137
Chandris	Mediterranean fly– cruise	10 days	134
Costa	East Mediterranean fly–cruise	10 days	88

£11,745 while the cheapest berth on the *Royal Viking Sky* was £13,035 which included a one-way flight London–Miami. Similarly wide differentials could be found in comparable cruises to the Northern Capitals, to Northern Norway and on the Black Sea fly–cruises. Such very wide price differentials could only be justified if there is a significant difference in the quality of product being offered. This is certainly the case. The Soviet hybrid ferry the *Leonid Brezhnev* is no match to the very luxurious *Vistafjord* on the Northern Capitals cruise, nor was the *Mikhail Lermontov* in any way comparable to the *Royal Viking Sky* for a round-the-world cruise. Certainly, CTC's marketing strategy as expressed by its marketing director, Eric Phippin, is 'value for money' rather than luxury (*Sunday Times*, 1 December 1985). This is reflected in its brochures and advertising material. Two years earlier he was claiming that 'people know we do not offer the same sort of service as the UK ships' (Seatrade, January 1984).

The price and product differentials are so wide that one may doubt whether CTC and its competitors at the top end of the market are really aiming for the same market segments. There is some overlap in potential markets but it is likely to be quite limited. Those passengers able to afford only the lower priced berths on the more luxurious cruise lines may consider opting for a better located berth at a lower price on a CTC cruise vessel. That they do not all do so must mean that there is an awareness in the market place that the lower price also means a poorer product.

In the second group of cruise markets, CTC's prices and product quality seem to be more directly comparable with those of its competitors (Tables 8.15 – 8.17). This is generally the case where these competitors are themselves targeting the middle to lower end of the market. Such competitors are P & O, Fred Olsen, Chandris and the Italian Costa Line. When competing against these operators, one finds that CTC typical prices for a berth in an outside double cabin with bath/shower and toilet are sometimes lower but at other times higher. It is likely that in cruise markets where it is in direct competition with operators such as these, CTC poses a much more serious competitive threat than is the case at the middle to upper end of the market.

8.5   The impact of Soviet cruise operations

The Soviet Merchant Marine is successfully competing in the cruise markets of the UK, Continent and Australia. Of the two main cruise locations, the Caribbean and the Mediterranean, serious Soviet competition is found only in the latter. In these segmented markets Soviet activity is solely at the bottom end of the market. This is because Soviet cruise vessels are generally old, poorly equipped and quite small. Conditions on board are barely comparable with those provided by firms such as Royal Viking Line, Cunard or P & O on its better ships.

Soviet cruises are relatively inexpensive, though in some markets there are a few cheaper ones available. The analysis of cheapest berths on selected vessels identified only two firms, Chandris and Vacation Liners, offering cheaper cruises than the Soviet lines (Section 8.4.1). Another analysis, considering prices for comparable cruise itineraries showed most to be considerably more expensive than CTC. But two cheaper ones were identified and a further two were found to offer broadly similar prices for similar berths (Section 8.4.2).

It is because of the low level of cruise holiday prices offered on Soviet vessels, that British operators have claimed that they are facing 'substantial non-commercial competition from CTC' (GCBS, 1984). They list four factors to support this claim:

1 CTC is provided with Soviet vessels at internally agreed transfer prices;
2 depreciation, insurance and training costs are borne by the state and seamen are paid a quarter of British wage levels;
3 fuel is provided at a quarter of world prices;
4 Soviet tonnage is being dumped on the British market.

The prices at which Soviet cruise vessels are chartered in by CTC are clearly an internal matter for the company. A later analysis (see Chapter 9) of commercial criteria in Soviet shipping suggests that Soviet vessel operators have various target indicators which they must try and meet. This is the case too with cruise ships. Soviet cruise vessels are often bought second-hand from West European shipowners and some of them are subsequently converted in West European shipyards while others are ordered new from Finnish or other foreign yards. It seems improbable that the Soviet shipping corporations are embarking on substantial capital expenditure, much of it in foreign exchange, in order to subsequently operate cruise vessels at a loss. It is much more likely that the low prices charged for CTC cruise holidays reflect lower operating costs than any deliberate dumping of excess capacity at uneconomic tariffs. The question then becomes one of trying to see why CTC's costs should be so low.

Most of the reasons put forward by British shipowners to explain CTC's low costs do not appear to be valid. Soviet bunker prices may be lower but they are not substantially so. Moreover, CTC sailing schedules frequently preclude or severely limit the possibility of bunkering in Soviet ports. For example, the *Mikhail Lermontov*, according to the 1984 CTC brochure did not call at a Soviet port during its charter period from 22 December 1983 to 26 October 1984. Thus Soviet cruise vessels operating in Western markets are forced to pay the going rate for much of their bunker fuel and in foreign exchange. Many of their operating costs such as port dues, pilotage, supplies, on-board entertainers and so on will also be comparable to those of West European cruise lines. Soviet shipping corporations do pay depreciation on their vessels and also insurance. Though it is true that they do not pay training costs this cannot be a major cost factor. The biggest cost differential between Soviet cruise operators and most of their non-Soviet competitors is undoubtedly in labour costs. Soviet seamen do get paid substantially less than their West European counterparts though more than some Asian seamen (see Section 9.5). Since cruise vessels are floating hotels they are very labour intensive. As a result, differences in wage rates between seamen of different nationality have a disproportionately large impact on cruise vessel operating costs compared to their effect on cargo vessels.

It would appear that it is the low labour costs above all else which explain the ability of Soviet cruise operations to be marketed at relatively low prices. But, as the preceding analysis has indicated, their prices are not always the lowest. Other cruise lines also using older vessels and cheaper Greek, Italian or North African crews can also operate low cost cruises. In fact, CTC has claimed that two Greek vessels chartered for its 1984 operations out of Cyprus were actually cheaper than the *Armenia* and *Mikhail Kalinin* would have been, despite being slightly larger (Seatrade, January 1984).

Nevertheless, it is evident that West European shipowners in Britain, Italy and elsewhere do perceive Soviet cruise operations as posing a serious competitive threat. The preceding analysis has clearly indicated that such a competitive threat exists but at the bottom end of the cruise market only. Here CTC may be diverting custom from other operators. At the top end of the market Soviet vessels cannot compete in terms of accommodation standards nor on-board service and their very much lower prices reflect this. There is little reason to believe that potential customers for luxury cruises are being diverted to CTC's 'value for money' cruises. If anything, the low CTC prices are likely to be generating entirely new customers for the cruise market especially among the elderly in the middle to low income groups rather than diverting potential customers from more expensive cruises. This view of the role of Soviet cruises has been supported by others in the industry. Royal Viking line, for instance, have welcomed CTC participation in the cruise market on the grounds that they, CTC, reached customers new to the market who might take a more expensive cruise second time round (Lloyd's List, 30 October 1984). From this point of view, CTC and other Soviet cruise operators might be seen as the 'Laker Airways of the seas'.

CHAPTER NINE

The Economic and Commercial Basis of Soviet Shipping

9.1 Economic threat?

Like other outsiders Soviet liner companies undercut liner conference rates. Though they are often accused of under-quoting by rates that are unacceptable to other outsiders, the evidence does not support this view. There are several instances on the North Atlantic, on Europe–Far East and the Pacific routes where larger and more dynamic outsiders have been underquoting Soviet rates. The question of Soviet liner rate undercutting should be put in perspective however. First, it is evident from the analysis of Soviet liner shipping in Chapter 5 that Soviet liner companies do operate as members of the relevant conferences on a number of routes and follow conference practices. Secondly, it is also clear that on several of the routes where they operate as outsiders Soviet lines offer relatively little capacity and often operate the slowest and least reliable vessels. This is the case with the Balt Orient line operating between Europe and South East Asia and Hong Kong. Its vessels are very small, relatively slow and provide only about 4 per cent of the container capacity on the route. The poor level of service offered by many Soviet lines compared to conference members may itself require a rate differential to attract trade. This is particularly likely to be true in markets where there is overcapacity.

The aim of the present chapter is to consider why Soviet

freight rates in particular markets are so low and how it is that Soviet shipping firms can maintain such low rates. These two questions are inevitably interrelated. This necessitates an analysis of the bases on which key commercial and operating decisions are made within Soviet shipping firms. While there are a number of publications dealing with the workings of the Soviet economy there is little published information available on the basis of decision-making within Soviet shipping. This analysis is therefore based partly on a series of discussions and meetings in London with Soviet shipping managers and several visiting Russian academics, and partly on published sources.

9.2   The Soviet economic system

Soviet shipping firms operate within an economic system which functions in a way totally different to that of the West. The rationale and method of working of the Soviet economic system have been analysed in several specialist texts, such as that of Professor Alec Nove (1980). An understanding of that system is crucial to an appreciation of decision-making within the Soviet shipping firm. It is not the purpose of the present study to provide such an understanding but only to pick out some key features which are particularly relevant to our analysis of Soviet shipping.

An important difference between the Soviet and Western economic models lies in the level at which major strategic decisions are taken and as a consequence of this in the role of the manager at company level. In the hierarchical Soviet system the activities of a firm can be influenced by a number of organizations. One of the highest is the State Planning Committee, Gosplan. Although this is itself influenced by the guidelines and priorities decided on by the Politbureau, it issues input and output plans at a general level. As well as being influenced from above Gosplan considers requests and propositions from ministries, regional bodies, party officials and senior managers. Its job is to 'achieve balance by cutting the total requests to a level which can be regarded as practical, and feasible' (Nove, 1980).

The Ministry of Merchant Marine or any other ministry while attempting to influence Gosplan, especially in pursuit of special projects, is itself receiving general guidelines from it. But it has considerable scope in planning how to follow these guidelines. Ministers and senior ministry or party officials effectively take on the functions which senior directors or board members would take within a large Western company or conglomerate. Planning, within the Gosplan guidelines, is done at this ministerial level. The manager of the individual firm whether in shipping or any other sector is primarily the executor of plans produced at the centre. He is given certain tasks and the resources with which to achieve them. He will also be given a variety of targets which he has to meet. But the system is very hierarchical. The manager may be given quite arbitrary and at times unexpected orders as to how to accomplish his tasks or how to deal with particular eventualities. He may have little room for manoeuvre and little managerial freedom. Managers of Soviet shipping firms engaged in bilateral or cross-trades may enjoy somewhat greater freedom by operating outside the close constraints of the internal Soviet economic system but they are not independent of it.

Soviet managers are operating essentially within a non-market economy. It is not market forces of supply and demand manifest through a pricing mechanism which determine key decisions such as the level and nature of investment. It is the centre which decides what needs to be done to meet certain national objectives or priorities. Because of the size of the country and the complexity of centralized decision-making, the centre may have difficulty in ascertaining needs except at a general level. It may not know what needs doing at the detailed or local level. The centre makes general plans and allocates resources to productive units to achieve those plans. To ensure that plans are fulfilled a multitude of targets are set for individual firms which are rewarded through bonuses and in other ways if targets are met. But the targets may be contradictory or may mislead managers. For instance, a given increase in sales in a year is a common target. This may lead a manager of a factory producing several products to concentrate on those products which he can produce more easily rather than those most needed to meet the planners' wider national objectives. In fact the manager is thereby responding to market forces in a non-market economy.

Targets set for an individual firm are numerous and varied. They will normally include one or more output indicators such as the value of output, value of sales or fulfilment of delivery contracts; some measure of profitability which is normally either total profit or the rate of profit on capital; and some indicator of labour performance. There may also be targets relating to the quality of supply of that firm's goods or services such as on-time delivery. A whole host of other specific targets may be set. These might include the introduction of new productive capacity or the achievement of new investment levels. Certain of the indicators are used to calculate, often using complex and almost incomprehensible formulae, payments by each firm into three 'incentive' funds. These crucial indicators have traditionally included the following:

the targetted increase in total sales;
per cent target increase in profits;
the target rate of profit on capital.

Firms producing profits and achieving their targets in these crucial areas are allowed to pay some of their profits into three funds. The first is the material incentive fund from which bonuses are paid to managers and workers for achieving targets. Payments into the social, cultural and housing fund are also spent for the benefit of employees but indirectly through expenditure on sports facilities, holidays, housing and so on. Finally, the third so-called incentive fund is for the expansion of that firm's production. In other words, it is a kind of capital reserve for funding future investment.

However, payments into these incentive funds should not be seen as a strong stimulus for firms and their managers to produce large profits. In practice, profits are used to cover capital charges and other fixed payments as well as payments to the incentive funds. The latter payments are calculated on the basis of complex formulae and do not necessarily increase if the profits achieved are especially high. Any profits over and above fixed payments and the payments to the incentive funds are returned to the government budget. They are not retained within the firm producing these high profits. In this respect there is a disincentive to increased profitability.

9.3   Planning within the shipping sector

In response to the plans and expressed requirements for transport by other ministries, the Ministry of Merchant Marine *(Ministerstvo Morskogo Flota)* determines the routeing of future commodity and trade flows, both internal and external, and the infrastructure to be used. It makes its own plans and investment decisions on the basis of these future flows of goods and commodities. In particular it makes decisions on the level and type of port investments required and secondly on the number, size and type of vessels needed for each trade. The ministry then allocates existing vessels and newbuildings to the Soviet shipping company which is geographically located to best carry that trade which may be internal coast-wise trade or international. In practice priority is given to international rather than domestic trade needs.

Such planning of future tonnage is inevitably long-term, usually three to five years, because of the lag between ship orders and ship delivery. Projected freight movements can be allocated to particular routes and even shipping companies in the expectation that the necessary vessels and tonnage will be available. There are undoubtedly instances when this highly centralized planning approach works well. Trade flows turn out as projected and ship capacity is available at the right place to carry that trade. In the shorter term problems do arise because Soviet importing or exporting agencies of the Ministry of Foreign Trade may buy or sell abroad without considering the transportation of the commodities being imported or exported. If shipping is involved the Ministry of Merchant Marine is then faced with the problem of trying to meet any unexpected short-term requirement for shipping capacity without disrupting its own longer term plans.

The planning process is two-way. While the ministry takes the longer term strategic decisions, the individual firms feed into the ministry their own plans and needs in terms of scrapping of tonnage, new vessels, vessel modernization, handling equipment or other problems at particular Soviet ports and so on. The ministry considers the proposals from the various shipping companies, which may be in conflict with each other and with the ministry's own longer term strategy, and decides what should be done.

For the individual shipping firm, vessel acquisition is the most crucial area of investment and planning. Newbuilding schemes are devised by the companies themselves. They pass through the holding corporations up to the Morflot technical board and then to the main board of the ministry. But there is no guarantee that these proposals will succeed. The ship-building department of Morflot will collect the plans of the shipping companies and, to quote the head of the section, 'make recommendations that will rationalise these requirements, decreasing the number of ship types and prepare preliminary specifications' (Seatrade, 1976). It is through this process that decisions and plans made centrally on issues such as regional development or projected trade flows influence vessel allocation to the individual firms. More importantly, investment decisions must be within guidelines on spending issued to the ministry from above and it is the ministry which provides capital for vessel acquisition. But although the final decision on the key issue of newbuilding schemes is normally out of the hands of the shipping company there are other means of vessel acquisition. Within strict guidelines contained in the Five Year Plan, firms are allowed to build up development funds. Although largely for improvement to existing facilities these have been used at times for vessel purchases. Additionally in a few cases bank credits have been obtained to finance new ships. One example in the mid-1970s was when the Novorossiysk Shipping Company identified a need for multigrade products tankers. Although they failed to persuade the ministry that the vessels should form part of a newbuilding scheme they managed to obtain bank credits and ordered six to eight vessels (Seatrade, 1976). A final method of ship acquisition is through a hire-purchase scheme which begins as a bareboat charter and ends with transfer of ownership to a Soviet firm. This scheme was devised by the chartering organization, Sovfracht, when it realized that the normal channels for vessel purchase were too slow when it came to snapping up bulk carriers on the second-hand market. The scheme was introduced in 1973 and is still being used. Thus, a Soviet shipping firm can at times expand its asset base without going through the main channel involving the Morflot technical board. Through using these alternative methods of finance, firms can enjoy some limited degree of independence from ministry control.

The more routine approach remains, however, for individual shipping companies to apply to the ministry for more vessels if they find that they are short of capacity or if they see new opportunities but the final decision rests with the ministry. Thus in 1984 when there were only three small Soviet vessels on the routes between the Indian sub-continent and Europe, Morline were anxious to acquire more vessels for this trade but were unable to do so. Izvestiya class vessels placed on the route by one or two Soviet shipping companies had apparently been pulled out to operate on more remunerative trades. This example illustrates that a highly centralized planning system tends not to be responsive to the needs of individual firms and their managers. This can also be seen in the arbitrary way in which vessels can be switched between shipping companies by the ministry in response to decisions about trade routeings. Thus the decision in the early 1980s to service various projects in Vietnam from Black Sea ports led to the transfer of Ro-Ro vessels, which had been originally destined for other companies, to the Blasco Oriental Line based in the Black Sea.

Centralized planning as practised in the Soviet Union would also appear to have other shortcomings. It does not envisage failure to achieve targets and therefore does not make contingency plans. The Ministry of Merchant Marine cannot plan for the possibility of external or internal factors disrupting the achievement of its own targets or the targets of other ministries. Yet delays in planning implementation, climatic vagaries or problems arising in other sectors may and frequently do disrupt planned developments. Vessels ordered and built for particular trades have at times had to be switched to cross-trading or to other internal Soviet trades because delays in infrastructure developments – railheads, ports or inland container depots – prevented the use of those vessels on the trades for which they were originally intended. It is remarkable that in a highly planned economy it was not till the end of 1976 that the Ministry of Merchant Marine opened a plant for the construction of ISO containers specifically for the shipping industry (Soviet Shipping, 1983). Earlier container factories had given priority to the needs of the Soviet railways. As a result the ministry had previously been forced to lease or lease-purchase from abroad virtually all the containers used in the shipping sector. The factory part of the Ilyichevsk Shiprepair Yard, is now producing about 5,000 TEUs a year but it is unlikely that the Soviet Union is yet self-sufficient in containers.

Perhaps the best example of the inability of the Soviet system to contemplate failure and to use some form of risk analysis in planning can be seen in relation to the production of grain. Because successive plans envisage target levels of grain production which would more or less ensure self-sufficiency, the Ministry of Merchant Marine cannot allocate some resources to building vessels that might be used for the import of grain cargoes. To do this would be to admit in advance that grain production targets might not be achieved. Thus virtually each year, for whatever reason, there is a shortfall in grain production and vast tonnages have to be imported. With few Soviet vessels available most of the imports are carried on foreign vessels (see Chapter 7 for details). Despite the near certainty that this will happen again in future years the shipping ministry cannot build ships to meet this projected demand. At the same time the agricultural ministry cannot reduce its own production targets and assume a significant volume of imports each year because this would assume a failure on its part. So despite centralized planning, Soviet shipping capacity will be incapable of carrying more than a small part of the Soviet Union's likely grain imports for several years to come.

Morflot's reluctance to build additional grain carrying vessels is particularly surprising given that some employment for them could be guaranteed. Successive five-year grain purchase agreements with the US and Canada have commit-

146

ted the Soviet Union to quite high levels of imports regardless of the size of the Soviet harvest. Even the grain harvest target for 1990, at 250–255 million tonnes, is below what is seen as the long-run objective of one tonne per head of population to reach the desirable level of self-sufficiency.

The inability to plan and prepare for a shortfall in grain harvests is the most extreme and blatant example of the inadequacies of a highly centralized planning system. There appears to be no effective mechanism whereby the ministries of trade, agriculture and shipping can get together to plan and co-ordinate their long-term requirements in a realistic way.

There may be other reasons why the Soviet's fleet of tankers and other bulk carriers remain relatively small and incapable of meeting the Soviet Union's own trade needs. One of these is that the Ministry of Merchant Marine is responsible for capital expenditure on both vessels and ports. It must maintain what it considers to be the right balance of investment between these two areas. Currently and over at least the next two or three years the emphasis is on port modernization and the development of new ports. As a result, the capital available for the building or purchase of new ships is limited. Another reason may well be the bureaucratic complexities and slowness of buying new or even second-hand vessels when they are needed especially if they have to be bought or ordered abroad. Vessel purchases have to be negotiated for and bought by the Ministry of Foreign Trade involving a slow and laborious process.

9.4 Target indicators for Soviet shipping firms

Soviet shipping firms have a number of indicators which are used by the Ministry of Merchant Marine to establish performance targets for each firm. In the 1950s and 1960s too much emphasis was placed on simple physical measures of output such as tonnes of freight carried or tonne-kilometres generated. This produced undesirable side-effects. Firms tended to ignore low weight high volume consignments even if they generated more revenue because they produced less contribution to targets expressed in tonnes or tonne-kilometres. Some Soviet shipping lines even went as far as chartering in foreign vessels at high foreign currency rates to meet their tonnage targets (Bakaev, 1965).

Since the mid-1960s in shipping as in other industries greater emphasis has been placed on revenue or profit oriented targets and less on measures of physical output. Tonnage targets are still used but only as one out of a number of targets that have to be seen together. For instance, firms engaged in Soviet bilateral trade have tonnage targets. Their purpose here is to ensure that such firms meet the foreign trade needs of the Soviet Union before switching their vessels to cross-trades. There are no tonnage targets for cross-trading. Targets are established by the planning department within the Ministry of Merchant Marine. The department's aim is not only to ensure that bilateral trade needs are met but it is also constantly trying to rationalize and improve the efficiency of Soviet shipping. A variety of targets are employed to try to achieve this latter objective.

From the Soviet shipping managers' point of view the most important targets and indicators are those related to revenues. Of particular importance are the unit revenue targets. The ministry's planning department produces for each vessel type a unit revenue target expressed as revenue earned per day per capacity tonne. This target is related to the average costs of each vessel type. The operating costs of a particular vessel type made up of its expected daily running costs and its capital costs calculated on a daily basis are converted to a daily cost per capacity tonne. The unit revenue target is set at this figure or higher to ensure that costs are covered.

The target revenue per day per tonne is a critical decision variable. Each shipping company must try to reach this unit revenue target averaging out its revenues on vessels within each type category. It may accept freights whose unit revenues are below the target level but only if it can compensate for the shortfall by higher revenues elsewhere. Inevitably managers try to move their vessels where the unit revenues per day per tonne are highest. Sovfracht, the agency responsible for chartering out Soviet vessels will inform Soviet firms having suitable vessels for a particular fixture of the freight rate being negotiated. The firms convert this rate to the appropriate revenue indicator and then decide whether they should take the fixture or not.

For overseas trade paid in foreign currencies or for cross-trading the unit revenue indicator is virtually the same. Foreign earnings are converted into roubles at the commercial exchange rates fixed fortnightly by the Bank of Foreign Trade (Vneshtorgbank). Here too there is a target revenue for each vessel type expressed as kopeks/day/tonne which has to be met. The target is related to the daily internal rouble costs of that company. If this is so the implication would seem to be that Soviet vessels will not go for foreign exchange earnings at any price but only if they meet their unit revenue targets. On the other hand these unit revenue target levels may be quite low!

There do not appear to be any revenue targets related specifically to the earning of foreign exchange. The reason for this is fairly straightforward. The primary objective of Soviet shipping is to meet the needs of the Soviet Union's own external trade. If foreign exchange targets were introduced they might induce Soviet vessels to leave bilateral trades and concentrate on cross-trading. At a time when there is insufficient Soviet tonnage in certain trades, a shift of Soviet vessels to cross-trading would merely result in more bilateral Soviet trade being carried in foreign vessels. Thus the foreign exchange earnings from greater cross-trading would have to be off-set against the foreign exchange costs of chartering in vessels for the bilateral trade. The Soviet Union appears at present to give greater priority to saving possible foreign exchange losses on bilateral trade, that is to a policy of import substitution, than to using its fleet to earn foreign exchange in the cross-trades. There are, nevertheless, for a variety of reasons discussed later many Soviet vessels engaged in cross-trading.

In addition to unit revenue targets there is normally a total revenue target to be earned from direct and cross-trading. Corporations involved primarily in internal trade have different targets. Apart from revenue targets there will normally be a profit target as well, expressed as a specific increase in total profits or as a target rate of profit on capital after payment of capital costs (depreciation) and interest. Though working

149

within a socialist economy firms, including shipping firms, are now expected to operate at a profit. This is an indication of their efficiency. If a firm consistently fails to be profitable it may well be closed down. This has happened in other sectors of the economy though not yet in shipping. It is the attainment of its profit targets and/or the total revenue targets which are most important from the point of view of the shipping firm's employees including its managers. Part of any profits achieved go into the so-called incentive funds. Through these funds profits are used to pay monthly or quarterly bonuses (premia) to employees throughout the year and for a thirteenth month's salary. One of the funds is allocated back to the firm which spends the money on social welfare and other activities.

Shipping corporations may also have a variety of other performance targets required of them. For instance operating vessels to schedule or minimizing the consumption of bunker fuel per tonne–kilometre. Apart from specific targets, a variety of performance indicators are also used by managers. For instance, one profit indicator is the profit per day per tonne of capacity. This is used by company managers and the ministry's planning department to analyse and monitor the performance of individual shipping firms.

It is clear that revenue and profit targets are a disincentive to undercut prevailing freight rates. In other words, the Soviet shipping firm is better off if the unit revenue it achieves is somewhat above its target rather than at the target level for two reasons. First, because it is over-fulfilling its unit revenue target. Secondly, because by so doing it increases its chances of meeting its total revenue and profit targets and thereby earning bonuses. But the firm must be careful. It may not wish to generate unit revenues well above the target level for this might induce the ministry to set a more demanding target the following year. This is the so-called 'ratchet effect' of planning from achieved levels. High unit revenue targets the following year might make it more difficult to earn bonuses. The shipping manager often has a fine balance to maintain. He must achieve his targets but he may well be wary of over-achieving. There is certainly evidence to suggest that Soviet shipping corporations will leave particular trades if the rates go too low. For example in 1983 the Arctic Line with sailings between Europe and Canada withdrew its UK calls because it found the rates being quoted by Sofati/CAST too low. Earlier FESCO, which had been operating into North American west coast ports, gradually pulled out partly in response to the barring of Soviet vessels from US east coast ports but also because rates fell to levels which did not meet Soviet unit revenue targets.

Nevertheless there will be markets where the unit revenue target of the particular Soviet company operating in that market may well be below the prevailing freight rates. Soviet entry will therefore have a downward pressure on tariffs especially in liner trades where the Soviet vessels may be outsiders. In liner trades there is the added complication of the multiplicity of commodity rates and consignments. In such cases strict adherence to target unit revenues may be difficult if not meaningless. The Soviet manager will try to generate revenue from a multiplicity of commodities so as to ensure that the average revenue per day per tonne meets his target. Depending on market conditions this may mean some commodities being charged much more than the target unit revenue and some a great deal less. In this respect they will behave no differently than any other shipping manager of an outsider shipping company who is trying to maximize revenue.

While as a general rule it would seem that Soviet liner companies have a clear interest to keep freight rates up – it facilitates the achievement of revenue and profit targets – they are prepared to drop rates to capture market share. Their ability to do so is determined by their own operating and capital costs which as suggested in the earlier discussion of cruise shipping are clearly lower than those of most traditional maritime states. They are, however, not always lower than those of some of the newer shipowners such as those of Taiwan, India or the Philippines.

Because of the nature of their performance targets Soviet liner companies have a clear interest to be inside conferences rather than outside them since this means higher freight rates. But they may also need to meet their total revenue targets and it is here that a clash of interests often arises with established conference members. In order to achieve their revenue targets the Soviet lines may want a market share which is totally unacceptable to existing conference members. Offered a share which does not ensure sufficient revenue, the Soviet lines are forced to remain outsiders though there are, of course, several trades where they have joined the conference.

9.5 Comparative operating costs of Soviet vessels

It would appear that Soviet shipping companies, whether in the bulk or liner trades, will not trade at any price, that is accept any rates no matter how low, but will only accept rates that meet their unit revenue targets. The latter are related to their perceived costs. But what is the level and nature of these perceived costs and how do they compare to those of fleets from the traditional Western maritime states?

In making an assessment of comparative costs, a major difficulty arises because one is trying to compare the operating costs of vessels within two quite different economic systems. Under the one, factor input costs are determined largely by the interaction of supply and demand for those factors but also by institutional factors such as trade union legislation, or the power of OPEC. While in the other the price of factor inputs is arrived at by considerations other than those of demand and supply. Essentially prices within the Soviet system are based on cost of production plus a percentage of the value of capital. But costs are liable to change continuously while prices are revised infrequently, often not for many years so there may only be a close relationship between them at the time of, or shortly after, a major revision. Soviet prices reflect neither the scarcity of the product in relation to the demand nor its utility, social or otherwise, however defined. Thus the price of steel used in shipbuilding or the price of bunker fuel does not reflect the scarcity of these goods nor their world price. Given the difficulties of comparing costs of companies operating within such different economic systems it is probably of greater value to compare the costs of the major input factors in shipping, that is of labour, fuel and the capital equipment (vessel) used rather than to try and compare total operating costs.

Costs in shipping are generally broken down into three categories: costs which can be assigned to a specific voyage such as fuel, costs associated with ship operating and costs related to ownership of a vessel. The operating costs category includes crew wages and other crew costs such as training and repatriation expenses, supplies and spare parts, repairs and maintenance, insurance and administration. Crew costs are generally assumed to be the largest single element of vessel operating costs. The proportion of operating costs accounted for by crew costs depends on the type of vessel and the nationality of the crew but for West European owned vessels it will normally be in the range of 45 to 65 per cent. For a 50,000 tonnes deadweight tanker under a British flag with an all British crew, crew costs will come to 50 per cent of operating costs. If the same vessel has British officers but Indian ratings, crew costs go down to 45 per cent (EIU, 1979). Crew costs on general cargo or liner vessels will be higher and may rise to around 65 per cent or more. Because of the importance of crew costs, countries paying significantly lower wages to officers and ratings would undoubtedly enjoy a major cost advantage even if all other factor costs were the same.

There can be no doubt that the wages of Soviet seamen are very much lower than those of their counterparts on West European or American vessels. In 1976 the Director-General of the International Labour Office (ILO) gave an indication of the very wide range of wage rates for able seamen in different countries (Table 9.1). At that time monthly earnings (in sterling) of West European seamen were about two to four times as high as those of Soviet seamen while United States seamen were getting paid seven times as much. While some developing countries were paying their seamen somewhat more than the Soviet Union, others were paying a great deal less. India, for instance, was paying its seamen only about half the Soviet wage. The figures in Table 9.1 should be treated with some caution since total crew costs depend not only on seamen's wages but on bonuses and other payments, such as social security or training costs, on crew size and on the exchange rates used. Nevertheless the table gives an indica-

Table 9.1
Monthly Earnings of Able Seamen, 1975

Country of registration	Monthly earnings of able seamen £	Index USSR = 100
United States	362–412	696–792
Norway (starting salary)	256–280	492–538
France (minimum)	198	381
United Kingdom	147	283
Greece	119	229
Italy (over 20 years of age)	110	216
Brazil	78	150
Zaire	69	133
USSR (1975)	52	100
India	27–34	52–65

Source: Report of the Director General, International Labour Conference, 62nd (Maritime) Session (1976).

tion of the kind of labour cost advantage enjoyed by Soviet shipping engaged in international trades compared to West European or American fleets.

The level of advantage can be gauged from the fact that in the 1960s the wage bill accounted for only about 20 per cent of the total operational expenditure of the Soviet merchant marine (Korsakov, 1966) compared to the 45 to 65 per cent mentioned earlier for European vessels. The Soviet's labour cost advantage does not appear to have diminished. In 1977 the Soviet Minister for Merchant Shipping claimed that Russian seamen were earning £117 per month (Guzhenko, 1977). In the Netherlands in 1977 the average wage for seamen (including overtime, leave, etc.) was £788 or seven times as much as the Russian wage. More recent figures confirm this general picture. The latest edition of *Narkhoz*, the Soviet statistical annual, covering 1983 gives the average weekly cash wage of workers in water transport as 252.8 roubles (Fairplay, 18 April 1985). An exchange rate of US $1.34 to the rouble would make this equivalent to US $339. This is a top wage bracket by Soviet standards, 'scientists' for example earn R194 per month on average. Conditions of employment for water transport workers (including those involved in the river fleets and shore work) include a 41 hour week and, typically, four to five weeks paid leave. But in addition to the cash wage, a so-called 'social wage' equivalent to about 40 per cent of this amount has to be paid for though not all of it is funded by the shipping firms themselves. As well as medical and pension benefits this includes, for example, holiday vouchers. Furthermore, some seamen can earn much higher wages. Advertisements for ordinary ratings to serve on deep-sea fishing voyages offer wages of R400 per month plus foreign currency allowances paid when in ports abroad.

These features, coupled with the absence of a realistic exchange rate for the rouble make meaningful comparison difficult, but it appears that although Soviet wages for seafarers are low compared with the Western maritime states they are high compared with other Soviet industrial sectors. Furthermore, it seems that Soviet seamans' wages are not as low as those of some Asian fleets such as those of India, South Korea or the Philippines.

The comparatively low wage rates paid to Soviet seafarers are partially offset by the relatively large crews employed on some of their vessels. Although it has been possible only to determine crews sizes for a few Soviet vessels the evidence suggests that crews can be much larger than would be found on comparable Western vessels. This applies over a range of vessel types and sizes and includes new vessels as well as older types. For example, a Soviet 8,500 tonnes deadweight vessel delivered in 1984 has a crew of thirty-two. Under the British flag the crew would typically be twenty strong whereas the Norwegians would probably carry only fifteen men. The 27,000 tonnes deadweight Soviet tanker *Dmitriy Medvedev* carries forty men and although a similar figure may have been found on British ships in the 1960s the crew would be fewer than thirty today. Soviet Ro-Ros as small as 292 TEU are known to carry as many as thirty-nine men, but a Norwegian complement would be as small as fifteen to sixteen. The smallest crew known to exist on Soviet vessels is twenty-four for the 10,000 grt Kapitan Panfilov class of bulk carriers. Most of the examples available are of crews ranging from thirty-two to forty-six men on vessels which in North Europe would be crewed by fifteen to twenty-five. Soviet crew sizes appear to be 50 per cent to 150 per cent larger than those of their major European competitors.

Soviet shipping managers accept that their crew costs are comparatively low but they claim that Soviet seamen unlike their Western counterparts share in the profits of their shipping firms. They do this primarily in two ways. First, they are paid monthly or quarterly bonuses out of any profits which are earned. This is in addition to the normal 'thirteenth month' bonus which is paid. Secondly, some profits go into the firm's incentive fund and are used to provide free medical treatment, free holidays, sports facilities and so on for the seaman and his entire family. There has been a trend increasingly towards benefits other than wages and these have grown at a higher rate. In the Lithuanian Shipping Company, seamen's wages grew by 22 per cent during the first half of the 1970s but in the same period economic incentive funds increased by 230 per cent and social/cultural/housing funds were up by 86 per cent (*Soviet Shipping*, 1983). If adjustments are made for this, the discrepancy in wage levels and real wage costs remains wide but not as wide as indicated by simple wage rates. Furthermore, labour productivity in Soviet maritime shipping is estimated to be 5 to 6 per cent higher than in two other transport modes, rail and inland water transport (Levenson, 1984).

There is a widely held belief that Soviet vessels benefit from their ability to buy bunkers at Soviet ports at prices substantially below those prevailing elsewhere. This has not always been so. In the 1960s fuel oil prices in Soviet ports were substantially higher than those in Europe, the Middle East or the Far East when converted into US dollars at the official exchange rate (Athay, 1971). Diesel prices were marginally higher. Following the fuel crises of 1973 and 1978–9, bunker prices in non-Soviet ports escalated dramatically while prices in Soviet ports lagged far behind. During the mid-1970s vessels able to bunker in Soviet ports did have a significant cost advantage. This advantage has gradually been eroded as Soviet oil prices are allowed to rise closer to world level and, more recently, as the non-Soviet dollar price of fuel oil has declined. Nevertheless, Soviet bunker prices are still lower than those prevailing elsewhere. However, if the very low crude oil prices of $15 per barrel or less seen in early 1986 were to be maintained then bunker prices in non-Soviet ports should decline sharply. But it should also be borne in mind that when engaged in cross-trades, Soviet vessels only visit Soviet ports infrequently. This is particularly true on many long distance liner routes such as Europe–Far East. Even when they are able to bunker in Soviet ports, such bunkers will only represent a small proportion of the total bunker fuel used by Soviet liner vessels in such trades. Thus the operating cost advantage of cheaper bunker prices is diluted and becomes fairly marginal. This is also true for the cruise ships operating in the Western market.

Finally one needs to consider whether Soviet shipping enjoys a further advantage in that its capital costs may be cheaper than those prevailing outside the Soviet Union either because the price of vessels are lower or because depreciation costs and interest charges are low in view of the way they are calculated. In the 1960s the cost of building tankers and presumably other vessels in the Soviet Union was higher than the cost in Western or Japanese yards when converted into US dollars at the official exchange rate (Athay, 1971). Since then because of the very much lower rate of inflation within the Soviet Union it is likely that the cost of Soviet newbuildings is now lower compared to the costs in non-Soviet yards. This is despite concealed inflation which does not appear in Soviet price indices and has been estimated at around 2 per cent per annum. On the other hand, the Soviets do order some specialist vessels from West European shipyards and they have also bought second-hand vessels, such as cruise ships, in the West too (Table 3.2 and Chapter 8 above). Not all their capital investment is in roubles and at Soviet prices.

Soviet shipping companies have depreciation policies which are not too different from those of traditional shipowners. The capital cost of vessels is repaid through the depreciation charges. Depreciation is normally over twenty years on a straight line basis and there is an additional annual capital charge, the standard rate being 6 per cent of the value of capital assets. The latter is a form of interest payment for the capital used. A twenty-five year depreciation period applies to passenger vessels. In contrast depreciation on Western vessels is normally over fifteen years. It is Soviet practice to cover major repairs out of depreciation as well, rather than to include them as a separate running cost. This means that the cost of major repairs, such as new engines, conversions and refurbishments are paid for by the ministry out of the depreciation funds. Repair costs aside, the annual depreciation cost including the capital charge is a form of annual loan repayment to the ministry for each of its vessels by each shipping company. Depreciation does not go into a firm's own general reserve to be used by each company in the future. It is a payment to the ministry which has to be met in cash terms each year irrespective of the firm's performance. In this respect the demands of the Soviet system are quite strict. Thus, while Soviet lines can probably buy vessels at lower prices than their non-Soviet competitors the depreciation costs are calculated in a broadly similar way.

There may be additional differences in the cost structures of Soviet and non-Soviet shipping operations. For instance, insurance cover for Soviet shipowners operates in a way which is different from cover for Western firms. Soviet lines do not normally have any hull and machinery cover. It is argued that the high level of navigational safety in the Soviet fleet makes it unnecessary to have property covered (*Soviet Shipping*, 1985). There are some exceptions such as for vessels on bareboat charter/hire purchase arrangements where the agreement with the seller stipulates that insurance must be taken out. Ships undergoing repairs in foreign yards are also insured for the duration of the repair. Again, the contract requires this as the vessel is temporarily out of the hands of its owner. Soviet lines choose to take out the policy themselves rather than allowing the repair yard to insure the vessel. Freight containers are also insured against loss or damage as many are on hire from Western container leasing firms. All insurance policies are taken out with the Soviet state insurance company Ingosstrakh. The lack of hull and machinery cover in most cases means that in the event of a loss the value will have to be written off by the shipping company. In the case of the cruise ship *Mikhail Lermontov*, which sank in February 1986, the second-hand value was estimated at US $20 million (Lloyd's List, 18 February 1986).

In contrast, liability insurance is taken out by Soviet shipping companies under rules almost identical to those followed by Western lines. Claims against Soviet firms are through Ingosstrakh but cover is provided by the normal Protection and Indemnity (P & I) Clubs. Although Soviet lines do not take out the broadest range of cover available, for example insurance against death or injury of employees is unnecessary as this is covered by state social security, costs for P & I cover will be similar to those incurred by many non-Soviet firms.

There are, therefore, small potential savings for Soviet lines in terms of hull and machinery insurance for owned vessels in normal operation. On the other hand, it is likely that administrative costs of Soviet shipping firms are likely to be comparatively high because of the top heavy nature of such firms. Not all the cost advantages lie on the Soviet side.

Overall it is certainly the case that the total costs of a Soviet vessel, even one paying for a substantial part of its voyage costs in foreign exchange, will be lower than those of a West European or North American vessel. Much, if not most, of this cost advantage arises from the lower labour costs. It is much less certain whether Soviet vessel operating costs are lower than those of some low cost Asian fleets such as those of the Philippines, India or Taiwan. What evidence there is, for instance in the Europe – Far East liner trade, suggests that the Soviets can be undercut by lower rates being offered by some other companies.

9.6   Foreign exchange objectives

The earning of foreign exchange is likely to be an important consideration for all countries that normally generate insufficient inflow of foreign exchange to meet their foreign exchange outflows. The Soviet Union is one such country and clearly in using its fleet in the cross-trades it is able to earn foreign exchange. But is this an overriding consideration in Soviet shipping policy which pushes Soviet shipping corporations to operate vessels even at a loss in order to generate foreign exchange? It is hard to reconcile such a view with the fact that the Soviet Union, by failing to build up its bulk carrier and tanker fleet, spends enormous amounts of foreign exchange chartering-in foreign flag vessels. George Maslov, head of Sovinflot, has claimed that in 1983 the foreign currency earnings of Morflot in both the liner and tramp cross-trades covered less than one third of Soviet foreign exchange expenditures required to pay for vessels chartered in or for foreign liner tonnages (Maslov, 1984). Maslov may well be exaggerating but it would certainly appear that if earning or saving foreign exchange was the primary objective of Soviet policy, then the Soviet Union would have built or bought second-hand many more bulk carriers or tankers.

Nevertheless, earning foreign exchange or saving it is an important consideration in Soviet trade and shipping policy. It is for this reason that when they buy goods abroad they frequently do so on an FOB basis and when exporting their own products they sell CIF. The aim in both cases is to determine the method of shipment and, where possible, to ensure that shipments are carried on Soviet vessels. In this way they should save foreign exchange on their imports and earn foreign exchange on their exports. The Soviet merchant fleet frequently fails to do this because it has insufficient tonnage to meet surges of demand. Thus while foreign exchange considerations are important they do not appear to be the overriding consideration in determining the objectives of Soviet shipping policy. At the level of the individual vessel, we have already seen when discussing targets, that even in relation to earnings in foreign exchange there is a target unit revenue expressed in terms of Kopeks per tonne per day which must be met.

In the case of the liner cross-trades there will of course be substantial foreign exchange costs before any net earnings can be achieved. Bunkers, port and handling dues, provisions and other costs will have to be paid in foreign exchange. So net foreign exchange earnings may be quite low unless large volumes are carried or freight rates are high. From this point of view Soviet liner companies have a vested interest in preventing rates from falling too low.

The Soviet view appears to have been that 'to build tonnage for the sake of earning money in an unstable world freight market, such as the one we know, would be a waste of capital investment which can be used in socialist countries for better purposes' (Maslov, 1984). Empirical observation would seem to support this view. With the exception of some cruise ships, the Soviets have relied on newbuildings to modernize their fleet rather than on buying laid-up or second-hand tonnage which in recent years has been so cheap. If their prime objective had been to earn foreign exchange at all costs they could have dramatically expanded their fleet in recent years by buying on the second-hand market at rock bottom prices. That they have not done so clearly indicates that other considerations are more important.

Finally it is worth noting that few if any Soviet vessels are laid-up at a time when total world laid-up tonnage exceeds 40 million tonnes deadweight. The Soviets have argued that this is evidence enough of the fact that their merchant fleet's primary purpose is to transport Soviet exports and imports rather than to cross-trade. Nevertheless, there is a sizeable fleet engaged in cross-trading and a policy of avoiding the laying-up of any vessel must in itself lead to too much underutilized Soviet capacity on certain routes with a resultant pressure on rates.

CHAPTER TEN

The Impact of Soviet Shipping

10.1 The nature and size of the Soviet merchant fleet

In concluding this analysis of Soviet shipping an essential first step is to highlight what have emerged as the key character- istics of the fleet. One of the most striking features of the fleet is its peculiar composition. No other merchant fleet has such a high proportion of non-trading vessels dominated by fishing boats, factory ships and research vessels. This means that the active trading fleet is in fact smaller than would be assumed. Only two-thirds of the Soviet fleet is involved in trade, internal or external, compared with over 90 per cent for all other major fleets. The large number of fishing vessels distorts average vessel size giving the Soviet vessels a figure of only 3,500 gross tonnes, two thousand tonnes less than the world average. Even when non-trading vessels are excluded the average size of Soviet vessels remains small. Furthermore, the fleet is rather old now as many of the ships were built during a period of rapid expansion in the 1960s. The overall impression is that this, the world's fifth largest fleet is composed of smaller and older vessels. There is a large number of smaller general cargo vessels and an apparent deficiency as far as several modern types are concerned, including gas carriers, OBOs and fully cellular container ships.

In seeking an explanation for this peculiar fleet profile one can turn to an examination of the demand for shipping services in the Soviet Union. Under Stalin, attempts at near self-sufficiency meant that a large deep-sea fleet was unneces-

162

sary. In responding to rapid trade growth from the 1950s the merchant fleet expanded quickly during the 1960s. Now the Soviet Union is a major trading nation but its pattern of trade shows strong localization. This seems to be true of most centrally planned economies particularly in their export trades. For example, 86 per cent of exports from the Black Sea and Baltic ports of communist countries go no further than Europe or the Mediterranean.

A larger proportion of imports come from further afield but the figures represent flows of a small number of key commodities moving in large volumes. These include grain from the Americas and Australia, sugar from the Caribbean and ores from Southern Asia. Of the major Soviet trading partners only Cuba, the United States and India require deep-sea trading links.

The implications for the Soviet merchant marine are clear. Soviet external trade requirements are for a large fleet of vessels suited to short-sea shipping operations. In addition there are specialist requirements in the deep-sea area for the carriage of bulk cargoes. Any additional requirement for deep-sea non-bulk shipping is, relatively, very small. Coastal traffic within the Soviet Union is also a major part of the merchant marine's business. It accounts for over a third of total tonnage carried.

Theoretically, through central planning, the Ministry of Merchant Marine should be in a position to match closely the supply of shipping services with requirements for trade. The Ministry of Foreign Trade, via its various agencies, is responsible for almost all imports and exports. The merchant fleet is also centrally controlled; most trading vessels are operated by subsidiaries of the Ministry of Merchant Marine. But the degree of centralized control and the success of central planning in the shipping context are both open to question. An example of centralized control in action was the creation of the Balt Orient liner service in 1980 which involved renaming an existing service, switching it from one shipping corporation based in the Black Sea to another in the Baltic, taking the best container vessels from two shipping companies and reallocating them to a third firm. The establishment of this cross-trading line, large by Soviet standards, could only have been brought about by instructions from Moscow. Yet, at the same time there are examples of a high degree of independence being exercised by some individual shipping firms. Even vessel acquisition without central resource allocation is known to occur through elaborate high purchase schemes, particularly for buying second-hand tonnage from Western firms.

10.2   The competitive impact in different maritime markets

Our analysis of Soviet fleet deployment (in Chapter 4) shows that very few vessels are exclusively involved in cross-trading although a much larger number appear to combine direct and cross-trade activities. 'Topping-up' a Soviet foreign trade voyage with cross-trade cargo appears to be an important element of Soviet shipping.

About one quarter of Soviet general cargo vessels and bulk and ore carriers are engaged simultaneously in both direct and cross-trading though among container ships and Ro-Ros the proportion rises to slightly over one third. However, the deployment analysis revealed that the best vessels in the Soviet fleet tend to be employed on routes to other Comecon countries or on liner services within the freight conferences. Of the largest roll-on roll-off container vessels, fifteen traded exclusively on the USSR–Cuba route during the period of our analysis (Chapter 4). Other larger Ro-Ros operated within the Australian conferences. It is only the larger fully cellular ships, eighteen all told, that were being used on non-conference liner services. But these were medium-sized vessels in terms of TEU capacity and generally much smaller than vessels operated by the conference lines. The Soviet Union's smaller container vessels are, in many cases confined to the short-sea trades.

It is in the liner market that Western critics of the activities of Soviet shipping firms have been most vociferous. There are several liner routes where Soviet companies are conference members or tolerated outsiders and where they appear keen to maintain conference rates. Elsewhere Soviet lines often operate as outsiders to freight conferences and undercut the rates charged by these cartels. The amounts by which Soviet lines undercut are often among the largest of any of the various non-conference lines, though Soviet lines are themselves at times undercut by Far Eastern operators. But freight rates are only one of the competitive features offered by a shipping line. As Sletmo and Williams (1981) argue the freight rate can be the least important feature influencing a shipper's choice of shipping line especially if high value goods are to be transported. Factors such as transit time, reliability, frequency of sailings and meeting particular specialized requirements can all be more important than price. On many of the routes examined Soviet lines score very poorly in these respects (see Chapter 5). Where Soviet liner services operate as non-conference competition they are typically slow, infrequent, unreliable and offer few facilities compared with many other lines. In addition it should be noted that the amount of Soviet capacity provided on liner trade routes tends to be quite small. On liner routes where the Soviets are outsiders their capacity share is often as low as 2 per cent and it is rarely above 10 per cent. Other major non-conference lines such as Evergreen and Yang Ming who offer considerably more capacity, with much higher service standards and often with equally low rates, represent a much more serious threat to traditional conference members than do Soviet lines.

The carriage of Soviet imports and exports is the primary function of the merchant marine. This is apparent both from the numbers of vessels so engaged and the fact that many of the best ships in the fleet are involved in Soviet bilateral trade. The Soviet Union succeeds in carrying a large share, over 60 per cent, of its own international trade due mainly to the policy of buying on FOB terms while selling CIF. In some cases, such as India, bilateral deals have been struck, splitting trades 50–50, but there are major trade partners, including France, Germany, Japan and the UK, whose lines carry as little as 3 to 25 per cent of their trade with the Soviet Union (see Chapter 6). There is no doubt that the policy of buying FOB and selling CIF has been used by the Soviet Union to capture a disproportionate share of its direct trade for its own vessels. The fleets of other maritime powers who are major trading partners of the Soviet Union have been the losers and their complaints of Soviet policy on bilateral trade are justified.

At the other extreme the Soviet merchant fleet continues to be totally unable to carry more than a tiny share of the massive volumes of grain imported by the Soviet Union. Such imports represent the largest single bulk trade yet Soviet vessels in 1983 carried no more than about 10 per cent of this. Their share will have gone up since but it is still relatively small. Large shipments of grain to the Soviet Union every year since the mid 1970s have required the chartering of a large number of non-Soviet vessels, many flying Greek or open registry flags. Even Western owners not participating in this trade have benefited to the extent that demand for Soviet grain charters have kept freight rates higher than they would otherwise have been. When it comes to Soviet oil exports, Soviet tankers are in a position to carry well over half the trade. But as Soviet oil exports increase, more tanker tonnage is being chartered in. It is a feature of most large fleets, such as those of Liberia, Greece or the UK that they are active cross-traders in the bulk trades. Surprisingly, this is not so with the Soviet fleet. While Soviet cargo vessels cross-trade actively in some liner trades (Chapter 5 above), cross-trading in the bulk trades is very limited. This is largely because Soviet capacity in bulk carriers and tankers is relatively small.

As a whole, Western shipping has benefited from the widespread chartering by the Soviet Union of vessels to import grain and at times other bulk commodities and to export Soviet oil. The expenditure, in foreign exchange on such chartering-in far exceeds earnings from cross-trading by Soviet general cargo vessels. But it is evident that British shipowners have been slow to meet Soviet needs for chartered shipping. Much of the shipping needed to carry Soviet grain imports in recent years has been supplied by the Greek fleet and by open registry vessels, a significant proportion of them beneficially owned by United States shipowners. British flag vessels have participated only marginally in this market. *Lloyd's Shipping Economist* estimated that in 1980 British vessels accounted for only 5 per cent of direct tonnage movements on the US – Black Sea trade and only 3 per cent of movements on the Argentina – Black Sea route. The comparable figures for Greek flag tonnage on the same routes were 45 and 42 per cent of the totals (LSE, 1982).

One of the most controversial areas of Soviet competition has been in the cruise market where they have been accused of dumping holidays on Western countries, predominantly the UK, at very low prices. Our analysis (in Chapter 8) shows that Soviet cruises are only found at the bottom end of this highly segmented market. The ships used tend to be old and small and standards of accommodation and service are low. Soviet cruises are relatively inexpensive though a few cheaper ones are offered by Greek and other companies, offering similar standards and, like the Morflot ships, generally benefiting from fully depreciated vessels and low crew costs. Soviet vessels cannot compete in the upper end of the market in which lines such as Royal Viking and Cunard operate.

The prices of CTC cruises are so much lower than those offered at the top end of the market that one might well argue that CTC is the Laker Airways of the cruise industry. It offers cruises of a lower standard but at a much lower price. In this way, like Laker on the North Atlantic air routes, it enables a much larger number of people, many of them retired, to enjoy the pleasures of a sea cruise. Many of these CTC passengers could not have afforded the higher cruise prices of other operators. CTC is clearly generating entirely new markets for low priced cruises and not merely diverting demand from existing cruise lines.

10.3   Soviet overtonnaging in the liner trades

In conclusion reference also needs to be made to criticisms of Soviet overtonnaging especially in the liner trades. Because of their lower costs Soviet shipping firms are able to underquote British or other Western companies. Their ability to do so will normally be constrained by both the cost levels of their vessels and more especially by their unit revenue targets. At the same time the Soviets face the problem common to many shipowners of overtonnaging in certain markets. Our earlier analysis of the composition of the Soviet fleet has shown that while the tanker and bulk carrier fleets are disproportionately small in relation to the Soviet Union's own trade needs their general cargo fleet is disproportionately large. The growth of the general cargo fleet was very rapid in the 1960s, partly in response to the closure of the Suez Canal and the boycott of Soviet trade after the 1962 Cuban crisis. Growth slowed down in the 1970s and has now more or less stopped. The emphasis is currently on modernising and improving the fleet rather than on expanding it. Despite this Soviet general cargo vessels are, as previously pointed out, generally small, old and often substandard in terms of their speed, handling equipment and so on. They are not very competitive and because of this Soviet liner companies have had difficulties in trading with these vessels on conference routes where they must compete against modern specialized vessels. Their difficulties have been compounded by two developments which have resulted in Soviet overtonnaging on particular routes.

In the first place the barring of Soviet vessels from serving United States ports after the Soviet intervention in Afghanistan in 1979 forced Soviet shipping corporations to redeploy vessels previously trading to the United States on to other markets. Thus FESCOs withdrawal from US Pacific ports forced them to absorb 10,824 TEU on other Far Eastern routes. As a result Soviet capacity on these routes rose by about one third. Inevitably this must have had a strong downward pressure on their freight rates as they tried to fill some of this capacity. Vessels trading on US Atlantic routes also had to be redeployed in this way, causing overtonnaging in other markets and again creating downward pressure on rates.

The second problem currently being faced by some Soviet shipping corporations arises from the strong directional imbalances in trade on certain shipping routes from the Soviet Union. The Soviet Union is deeply committed politically and economically to supporting the development of a number of states around the world such as Angola, Mozambique and Vietnam. Such commitments often involve substantial flows of freight of all kinds from Soviet ports to these states while return tonnage may be very limited or may require a different vessel type. There is clearly pressure to carry cross-trade cargo on the ballast leg of such routes as an alternative to returning empty. Thus the Blasco Oriental Line operates a Ro-Ro service taking Soviet exports from Black Sea ports to Vietnam. There is little return cargo so the vessels sail up to Japan, pick up some heavy plant destined for the Soviet Union but top up with cross-trade cargo bound for the Eastern Mediterranean. Another example is of Soviet exports to Mozambique. Again there is little return cargo so vessels are used to supplement the Besta Line service between East Africa and Europe. The General Council of British Shipping has claimed that Soviet vessels will carry East African exports at almost any rate. The Europe/East Africa Conference claimed that a northbound £1 million contract was lost as a result of Soviet rate-cutting in early 1985. Clearly the Soviets are under strong pressure to drop rates when they have so much empty tonnage in one direction. In doing this they may well be upsetting conference rates in those markets but are they behaving any differently from any revenue-maximizing transport operator in the West?

10.4   Objectives of Soviet shipping

In an economic sense Soviet shipping firms behave no differently from firms operating within a capitalist free market environment. They behave as economic theory suggests they should. They enter new markets by undercutting existing rates and once established they try to push up the rates and maximize their revenue. In liner markets, once established as outsiders, they will try to join the conference as full members or settle for intermediate status as 'tolerated' outsiders. In joining the conference they will try to obtain a dispro-portionally large traffic share as any aggressive entrepreneur would.

Soviet undercutting of rates is perceived by some Western shipowners to be a most serious threat in the liner trades. The Soviets' ability to undercut rates is related to their lower operating costs. But it is facilitated by established liner tariff structures which are not cost-related at all but are based on the principle of charging 'what the traffic will bear'. Such a pricing strategy, can only be maintained when the supply of services is tightly regulated and controlled which is the aim of liner conferences. This makes it easy for the outsider to undercut the higher rates and 'cream-off the cargo' which is exactly what Soviet lines and other outsiders attempt to do.

If rates are much too high in relation to costs they can be easily undercut whether or not the outsiders' own costs are lower. The Soviet lines do have the advantage of having lower costs as well but not because particular cost items, such as depreciation, are avoided altogether though minor items such as hull and machinery insurance may be. Their lower vessel operating costs are primarily due to lower wage rates (when converted into foreign currency at official exchange rates) and lower costs of other inputs such as bunkers (when bunkering in home ports) or lower capital costs of vessels. These lower factor costs appear to arise not through any policy of direct subsidization but from the workings of a quite different economic system where prices of goods and services do not reflect conditions of supply and demand, but are related primarily to the costs of producing those goods or services.

There may be other forms of direct or indirect subsidization of shipping by the Ministry of Merchant Marine or other government agencies but it has proved difficult to establish the level of such subsidies, if any.

While their cost structures are different and in effect lower Soviet shipping corporations do have to meet normal commercial criteria, though they are not expressed as such. Each shipping firm and by extension each vessel has to meet, as previously discussed, a number of agreed targets (see Chapter 9). These effectively ensure that revenues have to cover costs. As a general rule Soviet vessels will not carry on trading at any rates but only at rates which meet their target revenue levels. There may be exceptions to this rule, however, when it comes to vessels sailing back on empty return legs from Mozambique, Angola or other countries to whom the Soviet Union exports substantial tonnages (Section 10.3 above).

Cross-trading peaked in 1974 when it accounted for 39 per cent of total Morflot earnings in all markets. At this time chartering out of bulkers and tankers was on a much larger scale than of late and cross-trade liner services on routes to the United States such as Balt Atlantic were at a high level. Over the last few years cross-trade revenues have contributed

25 per cent or less of total Morflot earnings. These must be assumed to be gross figures and it is worth noting that net earnings in cross-trades may be quite low as non-Soviet port and bunker charges and other foreign exchange expenditures will be incurred at both ends of a route.

This decline in cross-trading is also noticeable in the volume figures. During the late 1970s thirty to thirty-eight million tonnes of cross-trade cargo was carried annually on Soviet vessels whereas in 1983 and 1984 the figure fell to around twenty million tonnes. What is more, cross-trading as a share of total trade has halved from 16 per cent down to 8 per cent over the same period. These figures support the Soviet claim that some cross-trading occurred because vessels were acquired · before they were needed in the bilateral trades. Cross-trade deployment was essentially temporary pending developments in trade or infrastructure which meant that the vessels were then required on the routes for which they were designed. As vessel availability for cross-trading has declined during the 1980s revenue from this activity has obviously fallen. A large increase in Soviet foreign trade carried in Morflot vessels occurred in 1982–3. In the late 1970s the level was around 110 million tonnes annually but more recently the figures have been as high as 137 million tonnes.

Finally, there seems to be little evidence to support the view that the Soviets are using their fleet as part of some grand design aimed at capturing major world shipping markets and at undermining Western shipping. In recent years the Soviet merchant fleet has grown relatively slowly and it is still grossly insufficient to meet the Soviet Union's own trade needs let alone pose any serious threat to non-Soviet trades. The earlier analysis in Chapters 3 and 7 has shown that the Soviet fleet is disproportionately small when it comes to bulk carriers and oil tankers. This view is supported by other independent analysts (LSE, 1982; Lydolph, 1985). The general cargo fleet is more than sufficient to meet Soviet trade needs. Though the bulk of it is engaged in direct trading, parts of it may pose a potential threat to certain liner conferences. On the other hand Soviet vessels are invariably older and slower than those of Western liner companies. They provide, as was shown earlier (in Chapter 5), a low level of capacity in TEUs and generally poor quality services which may well force them to offer lower rates to be competitive at all. If they were bent on rapid expansion of their fleet to capture a growing share of key trades, the Soviets would surely have been buying second-hand vessels in recent years when prices were rock-bottom. They have done the opposite. They have generally followed a policy of replacing elderly smaller vessels, tankers, freighters or bulk carriers, with newbuildings a proportion of which have been ordered abroad (Chapter 3, Table 3.2). The main exception to this has been the acquisition of a number of smaller bulk carriers suitable for grain shipment. They have concentrated on buying fairly young bulkers in the 20,000 to 40,000 tonnes range on the second-hand market. Though the scrapping rate for Soviet vessels has been fairly low, the policy of newbuildings to replace obsolete vessels has meant that the fleet has grown only slowly. Certainly such an investment policy would appear inconsistent with any primary aim of seriously threatening non-Comecon shipping. In fact earlv in 1986 the Ministry of Merchant Marine projected an actual decline in USSR tonnage of between 800,000 and one million tonnes by 1990. Despite further specialization of the fleet through additional reefer, Ro-Ro and container capacity, total tonnage would decline by 5 per cent (Lloyd's List, 27 January 1986). This statement was followed by the news that one million tonnes of tanker and liner capacity was to be scrapped in China during 1986.

If there is some grand design or ulterior objective behind Soviet shipping operations, the Soviets seem inept in pursuit of that design. Any adverse impact on Western and more especially United Kingdom shipping has been confined to a limited number of liner routes and possibly to the bottom end of the cruise market. In several liner markets where the Soviets operate as outsiders or tolerated outsiders, such as the very important Europe–Far East market, the impact of other outsiders like Evergreen or Yang Ming has been more significant because they offer considerably more capacity and higher service quality.

Criticism of Soviet shipping policy is perhaps more justified in relation to the bilateral trades rather than the cross-trades. This is because potentially the most serious impact for Western shipping is the imbalance of tonnage carried on bilateral trade with the Soviet Union. As trade with the Soviet Union grows the Soviet policy of buying FOB and selling CIF clearly undermines effective participation of vessels from the trading partners in this direct trade. By international standards the Soviet Union carries a disproportionately high share of its total international trade in its own vessels, despite the grain trade where Soviet participation is very low. Facilitating participation of non-Soviet shipping firms in the bilateral trades would go a long way towards removing a major cause of criticism of Soviet shipping policy.

Appendix A

Some Liner Services Operated by Soviet Shipping Companies

Company and line	*Route*
Azov Shipping Co.	
Asitco	Black Sea–Mediterranean
Asadco	Black Sea–Mediterranean
Azmed Line	Mediterranean
Baltic Shipping Co. (BSC)	
Baltcapas	North Europe–Central America
Balt Orient	North Europe–South-East Asia
Balt America	North Europe–South America
Balt Canada	North Europe–Canada
Besta	North Europe–East Africa
Balt Australia	North Europe/Mediterranean–Australasia
Baltscan	Continent–Baltic
Black Sea Shipping Co. (BLASCO)	
Blasco Indostan	North Europe–Indian sub-continent
Blasco Oriental Line	Black Sea–Vietnam–Japan–Mediterranean
Odessa Ocean	Mediterranean–Indian sub-continent–South-East Asia
Caspian Shipping Co.	
Mediterranean Caspian Line	Mediterranean–Iran
Danube Shipping Co.	
Danube Sea Container Service	Europe–Near and Middle East
Danube–India/Pakistan	Europe–Indian sub-continent
Danube–Mekong Service	Europe–South-East Asia

174

Estonian Shipping Co.
  Balt Levant   North Europe–Eastern
                                   Mediterranean
  Scan Levant   North Europe–Eastern
                                   Mediterranean
  United West Africa Service   North Europe–West Africa (with
    (UWAS)   DSR and POL)

Far East Shipping Co. (FESCO)
  Fesco Straits Pacific   Far East–Canada
  Fesco Australia   Far East–Australia
  Trans-Siberian Container
    Line   Far East–Soviet Far East
  Fesco India Line   Far East–Indian sub-continent

Latvian Shipping Co.
  Rinela   North Europe–Eastern
                                   Mediterranean
  Portobaltica   North Europe–Portugal
  Ricona   North Europe–North Africa

Murmansk Shipping Co.
  Arctic Line   North Europe–Canada

Appendix B

Definition of Some Shipping Terms

Bareboat Charter: A long-term hire agreement under which the charterer appoints the master and crew and meets all running costs.

Cost, Insurance and Freight (CIF): Terms of sale based on a price for an export which includes the cost of freight to the port of destination as well as insurance. Both are added to the FOB price.

Deadweight Tonnage (Dwt): The number of tonnes of cargo, bunkers, stores and so on that can be placed on board a vessel to bring it down to its marks.

Free on Board (FOB): The terms of sale for an export includes an undertaking by the seller to get the goods over the ship's rail where delivery and change of title takes place.

Gross Register Tonnage (Grt): The volume of all permanently enclosed spaces in a vessel expressed in units of 100 cubic feet.

Net Tonnage: Gross tonnage less space taken up by machinery, boilers, bunkers, crew and stores.

P & I Club: A mutual association of shipowners which provides protection from large financial loss to one member by contribution towards that loss by all members.

Time Charter: A hire agreement under which the charterer has use of the vessel for a specified period but the shipowner provides the crew and provisions.

Twenty-foot Equivalent Unit (TEU): The standard ISO freight container unit. Most containers are twenty feet long (1 TEU) or forty feet long (2 TEUs).

Voyage or Spot Charter: An agreement under which a vessel is hired to transport a cargo on a single voyage.

References and Further Reading

Aims of Industry (1983), *The Challenge of Soviet Shipping* (London and New York: Aims of Industry and National Strategy Information Centre Inc.).

Athay, R. E. (1971), *The Economics of Soviet Merchant-Shipping Policy* (Chapel Hill: University of North Carolina Press).

Atlantic Council of the United States (1979), *The Soviet Merchant Marine: Economic and Strategic Challenge to the West* (Washington, DC: The Atlantic Council of the United States).

Bakaev, V. G. (1965), Izvestiya, 10 October 1965.

Boehme, H. and Buck, H. (1976), *Die Schiffahrtspolitik der sozialistichen Lander und die Ordnung des internationalen Seeverkehrs* (Hamburg: Schiffahrts-Verlag 'Hansa').

Boehme, H. (1983), 'The organisation, management system and market behaviours of the Soviet Merchant Marine', in Aims of Industry, *The Challenge of Soviet Shipping*.

Business Statistics Office (1985), *Business Monitor MA8: Nationality of Vessels in United Kingdom Seaborne Trade* (London: HMSO).

CENSA (1980-5), *Information Bulletins nos 20 to 28* (London: Council of European and Japanese National Shipowners' Associations).

Croner, *World Directory of Freight Conferences* (New Malden: Croner Publications).

Department of Trade (1979), *Competition Facing Western Shipping Companies from the USSR* (London: Department of Trade).

Desai, P. (1982), 'Soviet grain and wheat import demands in 1981-85', *American Journal of Agricultural Economics*, vol. 64, no. 2 (1982), pp. 312-22.

Dewdney, J. C. (1982), *USSR in Maps* (London: Hodder & Stoughton).

EIU (1979), *Open Registry Shipping* (London: Economist Intelligence Unit).

EIU (1984), *Quarterly Economic Review of the USSR*, no. 3 (1984), (London: Economist Intelligence Unit).

Fairhall, D. (1971), *Russia Looks to the Sea* (London: Andre Deutsch).

Fairplay, *World Ships on Order* (various issues), Quarterly Supplement to Fairplay.
Fearnley and Egers (1984), *1984 Review* (Oslo: Fearnley and Egers).

GCBS (1984), *Briefing Paper: Soviet Competition in the UK Cruise Market* (London: General Council of British Shipping).
Graham, M. G. and Hughes, D. O. (1985), *Containerisation in the Eighties* (London: Lloyd's of London Press).
Greenway, A. (1980), *Soviet Merchant Ships* (Havant: Kenneth Mason).
Guzhenko, T. (1977), article in *Marine Policy*, April 1977.

Hanson, P. (1970), 'The Soviet Union and world shipping', *Soviet Studies*, vol. 22, no. 1 (July 1970), pp. 44–60.
Harbron, J. D. (1962), *Communist Ships and Shipping* (London: Adlard Coles).
Heldring, B. (1977), 'East–west confrontation in shipping', *Internationale Spectator* (Netherlands, November 1977).
H. P. Drewry Ltd (1975), *The Role of Comecon Oil and Tankers* (London: H. P. Drewry Ltd).
Hunter, H. (1968), *Soviet Transportation Experience: Its Lessons for other Countries* (Washington, DC: Brookings Institution).

Korsakov, E. (1966), 'The system of remuneration in the Soviet merchant marine', *International Labour Review*, vol. 94, pp. 398–414.

Lenin, V. I. (1950), *Collected Works*, Vol. 27 (4th edn).
Levenson, M. (1984), *Soviet Maritime Freight Transport*, Soviet Transportation Research Project, Working Paper no. 6 (Washington, DC: Wharton Econometric Forecasting Associates).
Lloyd's, *Export Shipping* (various issues), (London: Lloyd's of London Press).
Lloyd's List (various issues), (London: Lloyd's of London Press).
Lloyd's Register of Shipping (1972–83), *Casualty Returns* (London: Lloyd's Register of Shipping).
Lloyd's Register of Shipping (1984–5), *Statistical Tables* (London, Lloyd's Register of Shipping).
LSE (1982), 'USSR maritime implications of political/economic crises', *Lloyd's Shipping Economist*, vol. 4, no. 2 (1982).
LSE (1984), 'USSR fleet growth cuts chartering needs', *Lloyd's Shipping Economist*, vol. 6, no. 6 (1984).
LSE (1985), 'TSL: coming of age', *Lloyd's Shipping Economist*, vol. 7, no. 11 (1985).
Lydolph, P. E. (1985), *'Soviet Maritime Transport'*, paper to symposium on transport as a problem in the economic development of the Soviet Union and the communist countries of Eastern Europe (Berlin).

Maslov, G. (1984), 'Soviet liner shipping', *Soviet Shipping*, January 1984.

Morskoi Flot (1982–5), Soviet monthly journal on shipping (Moscow: Ministerstvo Morskogo Flota SSSR).

Moore, K. A. (1980), 'Development of USSR and CMEA shipping', *Greenwich Forum VI*, 1980, pp. 138–48.

Nove, A. (1980), *The Soviet Economic System* (London: Allen & Unwin).

Sangian, M. (1984), 'Freight Transit Operations via the USSR' unpublished thesis, Polytechnic of Central London.

Seatrade (1976), *Soviet Shipping: A Seatrade Study* (Colchester: Seatrade Publications).

Sletmo, G. K. and Williams, E. W. (1981), *Liner Conferences in the Container Age* (New York: Macmillan).

Smalley, G. (1984), 'Role of merchant marine in Soviet global strategy', *Marine Policy*, January 1984, pp. 65–8.

Soviet Shipping (1981–5), Quarterly Supplement to *Morskoi Flot* journal, vols 1–5, (Moscow: Association of Soviet Shipowners).

Stowell, C. E. (1975), *Soviet Industrial Import Priorities* (New York: Praeger).

Swayne, Sir R. (1983), 'The nature of the challenge', in Aims of Industry, *The Challenge of Soviet Shipping* (London and New York: Aims of Industry and National Strategy Information Centre Inc.).

UN (1984), *Monthly Bulletin of Statistics*, vol. 38, no. 9, ST/ESA/STAT/ SER.Q/141 (New York: United Nations).

UN (1985), *Monthly Bulletin of Statistics*, vol. 39, no. 7, ST/ESA/STAT/ SER.Q/151 (New York: United Nations).

US Department of Commerce (1967), *The Soviet Merchant Marine* (Washington, DC: US Government Printing Office).

US Department of Commerce (1977), *Expansion of the Soviet Merchant Marine into the US Maritime Trades* (Washington, DC: US Department of Commerce).

Vneshnyaya Torgovlya SSSR za 1983g (1984), (Moscow: Ministerstvo Vneshneii Torgovli).

Vneshnyaya Torgovlya SSSR za 1984g (1985), (Moscow: Ministerstvo Vneshneii Torgovli).

von Sydow, K. (1981), 'Are Comecon services unfair?', paper to *Liner Shipping . . . Survival of the Fittest*, a Lloyd's Shipping Economist Conference (London).

WITASS (1982), *Annual Report* (London: Association of West India Transatlantic Steamship Lines).

Index

For Product Safety Concerns and Information please contact our EU
representative GPSR@taylorandfrancis.com
Taylor & Francis Verlag GmbH, Kaufingerstraße 24, 80331 München, Germany

www.ingramcontent.com/pod-product-compliance
Ingram Content Group UK Ltd.
Pitfield, Milton Keynes, MK11 3LW, UK
UKHW021828240425
457818UK00006B/110